T0351689

THE PLAY OF DANIEL KEYES'

Flowers for Algernon

Adapted by Bert Coules

Notes and questions by
Robert Chambers

Heinemann is an imprint of Pearson Education Limited,
a company incorporated in England and Wales, having
its registered office at Edinburgh Gate, Harlow, Essex,
CM20 2JE. Registered company number: 872828

Heinemann is a registered trademark of Pearson Education Limited

Published in the *Heinemann Plays* series 1993

35

A catalogue record for this book is available from the British Library on request.
ISBN: 978 0 435 232 93 1

Cover design by Keith Pointing
Designed by Jeffrey White Creative Associates
Typeset by Taurus Graphics, Kidlington, Oxon
Printed and Bound in Great Britain
by Bell & Bain Ltd, Glasgow

CONTENTS

PREFACE

In this edition of *Flowers for Algernon: the Radio Play,* you will find notes, questions and activities to help in studying the play in class, particularly at GCSE level. The original short story, *Flowers for Algernon* is also included in this edition.

The introduction provides background information on Daniel Keyes and the writing of *Flowers for Algernon.* It also discusses the themes and issues in *Flowers for Algernon* and the implications of adapting it for radio.

The activities at the end of the book range from straightforward *Keeping Track* questions which can be tackled at the end of each act to focus close attention on what is happening in the play, through more detailed work on characters and themes in *Explorations.* The short story is followed by activities comparing the short story and the play.

At the end of the book is a glossary, arranged by acts, for easy reference, and Suggestions for Further Reading.

INTRODUCTION

Daniel Keyes

Daniel Keyes was born in New York. At seventeen, after a year at New York University, he joined the US Maritime Service and went to sea as a ship's purser on oil tankers carrying cargo between the US and Europe and the Middle East.

When Daniel Keyes left the sea he resumed his studies at Brooklyn College (now Cuny) where he received his BA degree in psychology in 1950. The following month he was employed as associate fiction editor by *Magazine Management* in New York. Here Keyes began to learn the craft of writing. He left editing to enter the fashion photography business, and then, after earning a licence to teach English in the New York City schools, he came full circle to teach at the high school from which he'd graduated ten years earlier.

While teaching days and writing weekends, Keyes returned to Brooklyn College at night for post-graduate study in English and American Literature. During this time, in 1959, his short story, *Flowers for Algernon* was published and won the Hugo Award. In 1961, after receiving his MA degree, Keyes left New York to teach Creative Writing at Wayne State University (1962–66). From 1962–66 he worked on the novel length version of *Flowers for Algernon*.

The novel, *Flowers for Algernon*, was published in 1966. It was Keyes' first novel and it won the Nebula Award. He has since written two other novels, *The Touch* (1968) and *The Fifth Sally* (1980). He is currently a Professor of English and Creative Writing at Ohio University.

Flowers for Algernon

Daniel Keyes writes:

> 'The idea for *Flowers for Algernon* came to me many years
> before I wrote the story or the novel. 'What would
> happen if it were possible to increase human intelligence
> artificially?' Charlie Gordon is not real, nor is he based
> on a real person: he is imagined or invented, probably a
> composite of many people I know – including a little bit
> of me. After a great many false starts I discovered the
> technique of the Progress Reports. With these three ele-
> ments: the idea, the character, and the narrative strategy,
> I was well on my way.'

Flowers for Algernon was first published as a short story in
1959 in *The Magazine of Fantasy and Science Fiction*. It has
since been reprinted many times in many languages. Daniel
Keyes wrote the story as a full length novel in 1966. Like
the short story, it has been translated into many languages
and is studied in schools and colleges around the world.

There have been many adaptations of *Flowers for
Algernon*. The film version, *Charly*, was made in 1968.
The actor, Cliff Robertson, won an Oscar for his title-role
performance. In 1980 the book was made into a dramatic
musical called *Charlie and Algernon*.

In 1991 *Flowers for Algernon* was adapted for BBC Radio 4
by Bert Coules.

Themes and Ideas

Flowers for Algernon raises many questions. Amongst these
are:

1 Is it 'better' to be more intelligent than others or should
we value people however different they are?

2 What are the consequences of tampering with human intelligence?

3 Should a human being be used for such an experiment, especially when he is unable to understand what might happen to him? What are the personal implications for Charlie Gordon, the central figure of the play?

1 The 'value' of intelligence

Charlie Gordon clearly wants to be more intelligent. He recognises that he is slow and that 'being smart' is something desirable: he likes Miss Kinnian 'because she is a very smart teacher'; he wants to be able 'to read better and spell the words good and know lots of things and be like other people'. He assumes that being more intelligent will be better.

However, other characters in the play who have more intelligence display weaknesses and problems that lead us to question whether increased intelligence makes us 'better' or happier people. Charlie is initially unaware of the prejudice that other people have towards people like him and the unkind things that they do or say. He 'wakes up' to a world that is far more hostile and imperfect than he could have realised before the operation:

'How strange it is that people of honest feelings and sensibility, who would not take advantage of a man born without arms or legs – how such people think nothing of abusing a man born with low intelligence.'

(From Daniel Keyes' short story)

Charlie's workmates patronise him, mock him and humiliate him. They laugh at his slowness ('doing a Charlie Gordon'), make jokes about him that he cannot understand and use him to provide a cheap laugh at social functions.

After Charlie's operation they change their attitude. After Charlie suggests a new way of lining up the machines on the production line (saving thousands of pounds a year in labour and bringing about increased production) he is given a fifty pound bonus by Mr Donnegan, the factory owner. However, the workers petition to remove Charlie. Charlie's intelligence threatens his workmates in two ways. Firstly, they cannot mock him and entertain themselves through their feelings of superiority over him. Secondly, his insights into greater efficiency mean that their secure jobs might be reduced in number. (It is interesting that when Charlie regresses, Joe and Frank support him towards the end of the play. Is this because their prejudices have been eroded a little or because they are more comfortable with the old Charlie?).

The professionals display different attitudes. Dr Nemur is anxious to leave a worthy legacy as a psychologist and Charlie may be his last chance. Charlie comments that Nemur is 'shackled by self doubt' and his inferiority complex is, ironically, fuelled by Charlie himself. 'To him I'm just a test result' he bitterly comments to Miss Kinnian. Dr Nemur ought to know better. After all, he is a trained psychologist; he ought to be far more aware of his motives for making this experiment a success and of the possible consequences for Charlie. It is Dr Strauss who accuses him of being 'more interested in (his) own glory than in the experiment'. Dr Strauss, the gifted surgeon, is far more sympathetic and understanding but shows some naivety. Has he taken enough advice from others about the possible consequences?

Miss Kinnian wants the best for her students but cannot have the expertise of the two doctors. What she offers Charlie is friendship, trying to cushion the experiences that he will undergo as his intelligence and awareness improve:

'You shouldn't feel bad if you find out that some people aren't as nice as you think'.

Above all, she values him for what he is – a person – and

doesn't make judgements about his value depending on his intellect or abilities. Her training as a teacher of adults with learning difficulties enables her to understand Charlie's difficulties and frustrations. Understandably, she is keen that he should be allowed access to a world previously closed to him:

> '. . . each step will open new worlds that you never even knew existed'.

but she is sensitive enough to look to the future as Charlie progresses:

> 'I just hope I wasn't wrong, advising you to go into this in the first place'.

eventually sensing his isolation: unable to relate to people and with the fear that the regression will soon happen to him.

Increasing intelligence – the implications

Flowers for Algernon also explores the moral, physical and psychological implications of man attempting to 'tamper' with Nature. Before we consider what actually happens in this play, let us suppose that the experiment were to be successful.

If anyone's intelligence could be trebled, what would the implications be? Would there be queues of parents wanting the operation for their children to improve their job prospects? Would entry requirements to any job or university be increased? Could governments control the population in a variety of ways (for example, keeping some people with normal intelligence as average workers, those with subnormal intelligence as manual workers doing the worse paid and least skilled jobs, and using the operation to produce a group of super-intelligent managers and leaders)? Or, what if a country were to operate on all newly born babies to produce a race of super-intelligent people? Could this increased intelligence be used in unpleasant ways against other countries? More sinister, would be the possibility of destroying people of weaker intelligence – a kind of selection through IQ – or destroying those who displayed too much natural intelligence.

Perhaps there is greatness in diversity; that is to say, all societies need to have the weak and the strong, the talented and the not-so-talented. Of course, striving to be better is important. But whatever happens, a civilised society must encourage tolerance, understanding and humanity. When these qualities cease to exist it returns to a primeval, dog-eat-dog world. Charlie senses this in the cafe when he sees the slow-witted boy drop the plates. He joins in the laughter and then is horrified:

'I was laughing at him. Just like all those others . . . it took that simple-minded boy to make me see the truth'.

Dr Strauss and Dr Nemur have a huge responsibility. Firstly, they have to think of the consequences for Charlie if the operation is a success. His life will be altered. He may be more intelligent but how will he cope with the emotional changes?

Moreover, he might be the isolated genius unable to relate to others. As he says to Miss Kinnian:

'I can't communicate with anyone very much, now'.

Secondly, if it works for Charlie, how will other people respond to this new possibility? Helping those with a low IQ is one thing; but there are obvious possibilities that such an operation could be undergone for other, less savoury reasons. Thirdly, if the operation is a failure what damage might be done to Charlie? We have evidence of his black and suicidal thoughts; and the spectre of Algernon's death is there too.

3 Human experimentation – the ethical dilemma

Should a human being be used for such an experiment? Daniel Keyes makes it very clear that other animals have been used before:

> 'He (Algernon) was the first of all the animals to stay smart so long.'

But has enough research been carried out? After all, Algernon actually dies during the play after his mental deterioration. Are the doctors right in operating on Charlie before sufficient testing has taken place?

Even if the experiment were to work on a human, can the subject withstand the later psychological pressures? Early in the play, even Nemur says:

> 'I simply don't think he'll be able to cope with it'.

At the height of his powers, Charlie bitterly comments to the two doctors:

> 'Charlie and Algernon', 'Algernon and Charlie' – two interchangeable experimental animals. We should be treated alike.'

It could be argued that Charlie is more isolated and emotionally starved at the end of the play than he was at the beginning. Before the operation, people talked to Charlie at the factory and at least he felt quite happy, and wanted. Later, his high intelligence creates a distance between them and him. He becomes more lonely. As his powers decline, he desperately tries to cling on to what he had.

At the end, he feels that he needs to go somewhere where no-one knows him. The pathos and irony of his situation are contained in one of his last lines:

> 'It's easy to make frends if you let pepul laff at you'.

Those in authority – Dr Nemur, Dr Strauss and Miss

Kinnian – regard the operation as a means of bringing Charlie some degree of 'normality'. However, we must consider whether any of these characters wants the operation to go ahead in order to improve career prospects or reputation, or simply to push wider the boundaries of medical knowledge and practice.

Medical ethics – informed consent

A patient's consent must be obtained before any procedure is carried out. This consent protects the doctors from any allegations of assaults (from patients who later regret the surgical intervention). The patient needs to participate in the decision-making process. This is relatively uncomplicated if the intelligence and the mental state of the patient are normal and stable. However, if the patient is unable to make an *informed* decision, there is clearly a problem and, it could be argued, a conflict of interests.

But have the doctors given Charlie enough information to make an informed decision about whether or not he wants the operation? He is told that the operation might not be a success and that the effects might not last. But these explanations are played down. In effect, Charlie hears what he wants to hear. Do the doctors go to great lengths to make him understand what problems might occur? Do these doctors *want* him to understand fully?

In Performance

As you read this play, do remember that it has been adapted for radio and is not meant to be performed on stage. The original story by Daniel Keyes is written as a series of progress reports – rather like diary entries. In this way, everything is seen from Charlie's point of view. His experiences, his feelings and the explanations that he gives are more compelling and moving for the reader simply because they are written by him. Imagine how much would be lost if the story had been written in the third person ('he', 'Charlie') and not the first person ('I').

This intimate, internal world is superbly re-created by Bert Coules who retains the progress reports as a series of tape recordings. Charlie Gordon appears in most of the scenes of the play and frequently comments in his reports on what has just happened or what has occurred at moments which are not included. The flexibility and the subtlety of the medium of radio are beautifully demonstrated in this script.

Robert Chambers

About the Radio Play

Radio, like film and television, is a medium where drama is shaped by a technology which has its own particular conventions, practices and jargon. Unique to radio plays (and one of the things which makes them relatively quick and cheap to produce) is the fact that the actors don't have to learn the lines and the moves, but can work with the script in their hands. This means that a radio playscript is rather like a music score: it's a performance tool which has to set out all the elements of the show so that they're clear and easily read, not only by the actors but also the technicians and production staff. At the same time, it also has to present the writer's ideas in a gripping and evocative way, so that a producer or script-editor can imagine what the finished show will sound like just from a reading of the text. It can be something of a challenge combining the two requirements.

A few explanations:

A *teaser* is a short scene placed before the opening announcements to hook the audience and possibly also set the mood and tone of the piece as a whole.

If a voice is *filtered*, some of the frequencies of the sound are altered – as with tone controls or a graphic equaliser. This can affect the voice quite drastically, making it sound, for example, as though it's being heard down a telephone line, on a public address system or, as in Charlie's tapes in *Flowers*, on a small cassette recorder.

Mic equals microphone. *Mic bumps* which are mentioned in a few of Charlie's speeches are something which you wouldn't normally hear, since handling a microphone clumsily usually produces very unpleasant and intrusive noises. In this case deliberately poor technical presentation is used to make a dramatic point about Charlie's co-ordination.

Int and *Ext* in the scene descriptions stand for interior and exterior. In a sound-only medium it's very easy for aural fatigue to set in, so a variety of settings is usually a good thing. Other ways of avoiding wearing out the listener include having scenes of varied lengths, and directing actors to work at different distances from the microphones. Speaking close gives a feeling of intimacy and confidentiality; speaking from further away feels more public and outgoing. Moving from one placing to another while talking can be very effective, particularly if the move is from off-mic to on. This is indicated in the script by (*Approaching*).

Out marks the end of a scene. Exactly how the scene should finish is determined by the director, whose job is to control the overall shape of the programme. As with microphone placing, different techniques have different emotional impacts: a scene can fade slowly, cut abruptly, overlap with the next scene, and so on. The beginnings of scenes can be equally varied, and one of the factors that most determines the overall 'feel' of a radio show is how the junctions between scenes are arranged.

That's all the technical stuff you need. One last thing: adapting another writer's work for a different medium is a daunting task which carries a fair amount of responsibility. When the original piece is generally regarded as one of the greatest science-fiction stories ever written, the level of that responsibility becomes positively overwhelming. When you read Daniel Keyes' story, you'll notice that I've changed the odd thing here and there; I hope you'll think that I've remained true to the spirit of the original even where circumstances (and the differing needs of a play over those of a prose piece) have prevented me remaining true to the letter.

Bert Coules

11 May 1992

The Cast

Character Notes

Accents are basically London/Southern England except where stated.

Charlie

Charlie Gordon, a mentally handicapped man with an IQ of only 68 who works as a cleaner in a factory. Charlie has a clear, if simplistic, realisation of his position in life and an intense motivation to educate himself. He is good-natured, gentle, trusting and eager to please. His speech at the beginning of the play is generally slow and hesitant, and is marked with a slight (and only occasional) stutter. This totally disappears after Charlie's surgery, but the moment of its eventual return, which marks the beginning of his regression, should be a key incident in the play – a horrible moment of realisation for the audience. Charlie is thirty-seven.

A note on the 'progress reports': in the original story, Charlie's records of his thoughts and moods (tape-recorded in the dramatisation) are handwritten, and the changes in his spelling and punctuation are a graphic indication of his mental rise and subsequent fall. The script retains the original presentation of the progress reports as the clearest way of charting Charlie's increasing and decreasing intelligence.

Miss Kinnian

A teacher of the mentally handicapped and other adults with learning difficulties. A patient and intelligent woman of great warmth. Thirty-four.

Dr Nemur

A leading psychologist and experimental theoretician, but a man who has never received the recognition from his peers that he feels he deserves. The Charlie Gordon experiment is his last chance to really make a name for himself, and he knows it. Sixty.

Dr Strauss
Dr Nemur's partner, a neurosurgeon and researcher into intelligence. More obviously humanitarian than Nemur, and more inclined to treat Charlie as a person rather than a test subject. Fifty.

Bert
A lab technician, assistant to Nemur and Strauss. West Indian, thirtyish.

Joe
A worker at Donnegan's factory, where Charlie is a cleaner. Not above making Charlie the butt of the occasional joke. Forties.

Frank
A co-worker of Joe's, and with much the same attitude to Charlie. Forties.

Mrs Flynn
Charlie's landlady. Irish, forties.

Ellen
A brassy, rather unpleasant friend of Joe and Frank's. Thinks it hilarious to get Charlie drunk and watch him make a fool of himself. Late thirties.

Mr Donnegan
The owner of the factory where Charlie works. No-nonsense and hard-headed. Fifties.

Professor Sherrinford

David Sherrinford, chairman of the World Psychological Association. American, sixties.

Man

In Miss Kinnian's class for slow adults. Any age.

Boy

A mentally handicapped young man, working as a waiter in a cafe. Twenties.

Owner

Of the cafe. Forties.

Customer

At the cafe. Male, any age.

Policeman

A policeman. Forties, fifties.

Man 2

A worker at Donnegan's factory. Not pleasant. Thirties, forties.

This dramatisation of *Flowers for Algernon* was commissioned by the BBC Radio Drama department in 1991.

It was first broadcast on Thursday 5th September 1991 on BBC Radio 4, with the following cast:

CHARLIE	Tom Courtenay
DR STRAUS	Barrie Cookson
MISS KINNIAN	Joanna Myers
DR NEMUR	Ronald Herdman
BERT	Clarence Smith
JOE	Nigel Carrington
FRANK	Alan Barker
MRS FLYNN	Auriol Smith

Other parts were played by members of the cast

Technical presentation	Carol McShane
	Hilary Carruthers
	Suzanne Howard
Production assistant	Jocelyn Boxall
Produced & directed by	Matthew Walters

In the 1992 Sony Radio Awards, Tom Courtenay was voted Best Actor for his performance in *Flowers for Algernon.*

DANIEL KEYES

FLOWERS FOR ALGERNON

Dramatised for radio by
Bert Coules

TEASER We're listening to a recording.

The sound is filtered, but not too aggressively – we'll be listening to these tapes quite a lot throughout the play. The recording begins with mic bumps, and the first words are much too close and distorted. Then things settle down.

CHARLIE (*tape*): Hello? Hello, hello. (*He gathers his thoughts*) My name is Charlie Gordon. I am 37 years old and two weeks ago was my birthday. Miss Kinnian says I shud say about what I think and evrey thing that happins to me from now on. I dont know why but she says its importint so they will see if they will use me. I hope they use me. Miss Kinnian says maybe they can make me smart. I want to be smart. I have nuthing more to say now.

A moment or two of tape hiss and room atmosphere. More mic bumps. Then a clunk as the recording ends. Music. Opening announcements. The music fades into:

SCENE 1 *Int: Dr Strauss' room at the hospital.*

We are listening to the end of Charlie's tape.

CHARLIE (*tape*): . . . . maybe they can make me smart. I want to be smart. I have nuthing more to say now.

DR STRAUSS *switches off the tape.*

MISS K Well, doctor?

DR NEMUR I don't know.

MISS K Dr Strauss?

DR STRAUSS How long did it take him to learn to work the recorder?

MISS K Not long.

DR NEMUR How long, Miss Kinnian?

MISS K Three sessions.

NEMUR *looks at some notes.*

DR NEMUR IQ, sixty-eight . . . Muscular co-ordination?

MISS K	Average for his development. Perhaps slightly above.
	STRAUSS *also consults notes.*
DR STRAUSS	I'd like to do some basic tests before we finally decide.
DR NEMUR	I'm not in favour.
DR STRAUSS	We'll do some tests.
	Out.

SCENE 2 *Int: Another, smaller room.*

CHARLIE *waits, humming tunelessly to himself. Finally, the door opens. He jumps a little.*

BERT	(*Approaching*): You must be Charlie.
	BERT *dumps a pile of cards on the table and sorts through them briskly.*
CHARLIE	I'm Charlie.
BERT	My name's Bert.
CHARLIE	How do you do, Bert?

This unexpected formal politeness makes BERT *stop his shuffling and look at* CHARLIE *properly for the first time.*

BERT	I'm very well, thanks. Now, Charlie – are you ready? I want you to look at these cards.
	Out.
CHARLIE	(*tape*): I had a test today. I think I faled it, and I think that maybe now they wont use me. What happind is a nice young man was in the room and he had some white cards with ink spilled all over them. He sed Charlie what do you see on this card. I was very skared even tho I had my rabits foot in my pockit because when I was a kid I always faled tests in school and I spilled ink to.

I told him I saw a inkblot but he wantid me to say what was in the ink. I dint see nuthing in the ink but he said there was picturs there. Other pepul saw some picturs. I couldn't see any picturs. I reely tryed to see. I said please let me try agen. Ill get it in a

few minits becaus Im not so fast somtimes. Im a
slow reeder too in Miss Kinnians class for slow
adults but Im trying very hard.

I dont think I passd the test.

SCENE 3 *Int:* DR STRAUSS' *room.*

DR STRAUSS Charlie, hello.

CHARLIE Hello.

DR STRAUSS I'm Dr Strauss and this –

CHARLIE (*memorising*): Dr Strauss . . .

DR STRAUSS And this is Dr Nemur.

CHARLIE Nemur . . . How do you do?

DR NEMUR Sit down please.

CHARLIE Right . . .

He sits.

DR STRAUSS Now, we have the results of the test you took
yesterday . . .

CHARLIE I couldn't see the pictures. I'm really sorry.

DR STRAUSS It doesn't matter.

CHARLIE There was ink all over the cards when he gave them
to me. I didn't spill it.

DR NEMUR Tell us about the night school you go to.

CHARLIE Miss Kinnian never gives me tests like that one.

DR STRAUSS How did you find the night school, Charlie? Did
someone tell you to go there?

CHARLIE No. I asked people where I should go to learn to
read and spell good. And they told me there.

DR STRAUSS Miss Kinnian tells us you're her star pupil.

CHARLIE *stares blankly at him.*

DR NEMUR Her best pupil. (*A moment*) Why did you want to
learn to read and to spell?

CHARLIE Because all my life I wanted not to be stupid. Are
you going to use me?

DR STRAUSS	Do you know that it will probably be temporary?
CHARLIE	Yes. Miss Kinnian told me. I don't care if it hurts.
	Out.
CHARLIE	(*tape*): Dr Strauss and Dr Nemur said that maybe they will still use me. They said that Miss Kinnian told them I was the bestest pupil in her class becaus I tryed the hardist and I reely wantid to lern. They said Ive got to go bak tomorrow and do some more tests. Praps Ill meet my frend Bert again. This time Ill try reely hard to see the pictures.
SCENE 4	*Int: A corridor at the hospital.*
	CHARLIE *and* BERT *walk along, steps echoing.*
CHARLIE	Where are we going?
BERT	Don't be scared, Charlie.
CHARLIE	I'm not scared. Will Miss Kinnian be there?
BERT	Not today. I'm taking you to meet Algernon.
CHARLIE	Al-ger-non.
	Out.
SCENE 5	*Int: A laboratory.*
BERT	There he is.
	CHARLIE *laughs.*
CHARLIE	Al-ger-non.
BERT	Algernon.
CHARLIE	Algernon.
BERT	That's right. You and Algernon are going to play a game.
	CHARLIE *laughs.*
CHARLIE	How can he play a game? He's just a mouse.
	Out.
CHARLIE	(*tape*): The game wasnt reely a game. It was like a race. Bert put Algernon in a box with a lot of twists and turns like all kinds of walls and then he gave me a pencil and a paper with lines and lots of boxes. On one side it said START and on the other

end it said FINISH. Bert said it was *amazed* and that Algernon and me had the same *amazed* to do. I dint see howe we could have the same *amazed* if Algernon had a box and I had a paper but I dint say nothing. Anyway there wasnt time because the race started.

Bert had a watch he was trying to hide so I woudnt see it so I tryed not to look and that made me nervus. Anyway that test made me feel even worser than the other one because we did it over 10 times with difernt *amazeds* and Algernon won every time. I dint know that mice were so smart. Maybe thats because Algernon is a white mouse. Maybe white mice are smarter than other mice.

SCENE 6	*Int:* DR STRAUSS' *room.*

DR STRAUSS	What have you got against him?
DR NEMUR	I just don't think he's the right candidate.
DR STRAUSS	Oh, that's a very scientific argument.
DR NEMUR	Look, we're making history here. If the operation succeeds . . .
DR STRAUSS	If it succeeds, you'll have your place in the history books whoever the subject is.
DR NEMUR	You think that's all I care about?
DR STRAUSS	I know Charlie isn't exactly what you had in mind for the first of your new breed.
DR NEMUR	New breed! You make me sound like some kind of Frankenstein. Look, all the indications are for a tripling of base intelligence at the very least. I simply don't think he'll be able to cope with it.
	Out.
CHARLIE	*(tape)*: Their going to use me! Im so exited. Dr Nemur and Dr Strauss had a argament about it first. I heard them from outside the door. I dint get all the words and they were talking to fast but it sounded like Dr Strauss was on my side and like the other one wasnt. Dr Strauss mustav wun. Their not

here now. They've gone. Im waiting for Miss Kinnian to take me home. I like Miss Kinnian becaus shes a very smart teacher.

SCENE 7 *Ext: A street. Night.*

MISS K Well, Charlie. You're going to have a second chance. How do you feel?

CHARLIE I'm scared. I never had an operation before.

MISS K Dr Strauss is a very fine surgeon. You'll be in good hands.

CHARLIE What about Dr Nemur? He doesn't like me.

MISS K Now I'm sure that's not true. But he can't operate on you, Charlie. He's a psychologist.

CHARLIE Psy . . . ?

MISS K He's a doctor who knows about how you think.

CHARLIE If he knows how I think, he knows I don't like him either. I'm scared.

MISS K Oh Charlie, don't be scared. You've done so much with so little. I think you deserve this more than anybody.

Out.

CHARLIE (*tape*): Dr Strauss said I had something that was very good. He said I had a good motor-vation. I never even knew I had that. I felt proud when he said that not every body with an eye-q of 68 had that thing. I dont know what it is or where I got it but he said Algernon had it too. Algernons motor-vation is the cheese they put in his box. But it cant be that because I didnt eat any cheese this week.

SCENE 8 *Int: A hospital ward.*

We listen for a moment to the usual echoing background noises. CHARLIE has been prepped for his operation and is very sleepy.

DR STRAUSS (*Approaching*): Hello Charlie.

CHARLIE Hello, Dr Strauss.

DR STRAUSS *puts down the equipment he was carrying.*

Through the following dialogue, he prepares to give CHARLIE *an injection.*

DR STRAUSS Are you feeling sleepy?

CHARLIE Yes. Dr Nemur took my sweets away.

DR STRAUSS Your sweets?

CHARLIE The nurses gave me a box of sweets. And Miss Kinnian gave me a card, see? It says 'Good luck'. And inside it says 'love from Miss Kinnian'. Lots of people have come to wish me luck. I hope I have luck.

DR STRAUSS Are you scared, Charlie?

CHARLIE I've got my rabbit's foot and my lucky penny. Dr Strauss?

DR STRAUSS Yes?

CHARLIE After the operation . . . After the operation will I beat Algernon in the race?

DR STRAUSS Maybe.

CHARLIE If the operation works, I'll show that mouse I can be as smart as he is. Maybe smarter.

DR STRAUSS That's the spirit.

CHARLIE Then I'll be able to read better and spell the words good and know lots of things and be like other people. What's that?

DR STRAUSS It's just something to make you sleep. An injection.

CHARLIE No! It'll hurt.

DR STRAUSS No it won't.

CHARLIE Yes it will. I already had one.

DR STRAUSS This is the last one. Relax, now. It won't hurt, Charlie. Trust me.

CHARLIE All right . . .

DR STRAUSS That's the way . . .

CHARLIE *flinches as the needle goes in.*

That's it. All over.

CHARLIE You said it wouldn't hurt. You said . . .

He's out.
The background fades.
Music. It takes us to:

SCENE 9 *Int: A private room.*

CHARLIE *is gradually coming round.*
MISS KINNIAN*'s voice starts in heavy echo and slowly comes into focus.*
As it does, we become aware of the regular electronic beeping of monitoring devices.

MISS K Charlie? Charlie? Can you hear me? Can you hear me?

DR STRAUSS Wake up Charlie.

CHARLIE *groans as he partly surfaces.*

MISS K Hello Charlie.

CHARLIE Miss Kinnian?

MISS K That's right.

CHARLIE Where are you? I can't see! I can't see anything!

DR STRAUSS There are bandages on your eyes.

CHARLIE What happened?

MISS K The operation's over, Charlie. It's all over.

CHARLIE Am I smart, now?

DR STRAUSS Go back to sleep. I'll come and see you again soon.

CHARLIE (*falling asleep again*): Did it work? Am I smart? Am I smart now . . . ?

His breathing becomes regular. A moment.

MISS K Well, doctor?

DR STRAUSS We can't possibly know straight away. We'll get a better idea in a couple of days, after Nemur's had a few chats with him.

Out.
From this point, CHARLIE*'s stutter begins to gradually disappear.*

CHARLIE (*tape*): The operashun dint hurt. He did it while I was sleeping. They took off the bandijis from my eyes and my head today so I can make another tape. Dr Nemur sayd there called PROGRESS REPORTS. He says its OK to tell about all the things that happin to me but he says I should tell more about what I feel and what I think. When I told him I dont know how to think he said try. All the time when the bandijis were on my eyes I tryed to think. Nothing happened. I dont know what to think about. Maybe if I ask Dr Strauss he will tell me how I can think now that Im suppose to get smart. What do smart people think about. Fancy things I suppose. I wish I knew some fancy things alredy.

Scene 10	*Int: The laboratory.*

BERT *is entering data at a computer terminal. The keys clatter.*

BERT All right . . . Maze M-17A . . . Run six.

He presses a final key. The machine bleeps. A brief burst of print-out.

Here you go, Charlie.

He holds out a sheet of paper.
CHARLIE *doesn't take it. A moment.*

Charlie? What's the matter?

CHARLIE I don't want to play.

BERT Come on, Charlie. You've got to. (*A moment*) Algernon wants to, look.

CHARLIE Course he does. He always wins.

BERT Well, maybe not this time, eh?

BERT *puts the paper in front of* CHARLIE.

Come on.

Out.

CHARLIE (*tape*): Nothing is happining. I hate that mouse. He beats me every time. Dr Strauss said I got to play those games. And he said some time I got to take that test again. Those inkblots are stupid. There arnt any pictures. I like to draw pictures but I wont make up lies.

I got a headache from trying to think so much. I thot Dr Strauss was my frend but he dont help me. He dont tell me what to think or when Ill get smart. Miss Kinnian dint come to see me. I think making these progress reports is stupid too.

SCENE 11 *Int:* DR STRAUSS' *room.*

DR STRAUSS Now Charlie, you mustn't get discouraged.

CHARLIE But you said I'd be smart.

DR NEMUR We said you *might* be smarter than you were.

CHARLIE Well, I'm not.

DR STRAUSS It takes time, Charlie. It's only two weeks since you had the surgery. It took a long time for Algernon.

CHARLIE Algernon? He had the same operation as me?

DR NEMUR Of course he did.

DR STRAUSS Didn't anyone tell you that?

CHARLIE No! So he's not just an ordinary mouse!

DR STRAUSS Charlie, Algernon's intelligence is three times what it used to be.

CHARLIE But that's great! I bet I could do that *amazed* faster than an ordinary mouse.

DR STRAUSS I'm sure you could.

CHARLIE Maybe one day I'll beat Algernon. Wouldn't that be something? (*A moment*) Dr Strauss?

DR STRAUSS Yes, Charlie?

CHARLIE Is Algernon going to stay smart permanent?

Out.

CHARLIE (*tape*): Im going back to work at the factery. They said I shud go back to work but I cant tell anyone what the operashun was for and I have to come to the hospitil for an hour evry night after work.
Theyre gonta pay me mony every month for lerning to be smart.

Im glad Im going back to work because I miss my job and all my friends and all the fun we have there.

Machinery, activity.
Close, CHARLIE *is mopping the floor, singing tunelessly to himself.*

JOE Hey, Charlie, let's have a look at your operation.

Laughter. Several men and women have gathered. CHARLIE *stops mopping, anxious to please.*

CHARLIE Here. See?

FRANK What'd they do, Charlie, put some brains in?

More laughter.

CHARLIE I'm not allowed to say.

JOE I don't think he had no operation.

CHARLIE I did!

JOE Nah. I think he forgot his key and opened his door the hard way.

Everybody laughs.
Slowly, CHARLIE *joins in.*
The laughter fades.

CHARLIE (*tape*): We had a lot of fun at the factery today. Joe and Frank reely made me laff. Their my friends and they like me. Sometimes somebody will say hey look at Joe or Frank he really dun a Charlie Gordon. I dont know why they say that but they always laff. This morning the 4 man used my name when he shouted at Leroy the office boy. Leroy lost a packige. He said Leroy for godsake what are you trying to be a Charlie Gordon. I dont understand why he said that. I never lost any packiges.

The TV is on.
A knock at the door. No response.
Louder knocks.

CHARLIE Who is it? Just a minute.

He turns down the sound.

Come in.

The door opens.

MRS FLYNN Charlie you shouldn't have that thing so loud.

CHARLIE I'm sorry, Mrs Flynn. Have you come for the rent?

MRS FLYNN You paid me the rent two days ago.

CHARLIE Oh. Good.

MRS FLYNN You've got a visitor. Tidy yourself up a bit. (*Turning off*) In here, sir.

DR STRAUSS (*entering*): Thank you. (*A moment, then pointedly*) Thank you.

MRS FLYNN Right.

She goes, closing the door.

A moment.

DR STRAUSS (*approaching*): Hello Charlie.

CHARLIE (*a mumble*): Hello, Dr Strauss.

DR STRAUSS May I sit down?

No response. He draws up a chair and sits.

Charlie, why didn't you come to the hospital tonight? (*A moment*) You know you're supposed to come every night, don't you.

CHARLIE I don't want to come no more.

DR STRAUSS Why not?

CHARLIE I don't like to race with Algernon.

DR STRAUSS Ah. Because you always lose?

CHARLIE How would you like it if you got beat by a mouse?

DR STRAUSS I wouldn't like it at all.

CHARLIE No.

DR STRAUSS I'll tell you what. You don't have to race Algernon for a while. How's that?

CHARLIE No more races?

DR STRAUSS Not for the moment. But I would like you to come in after work every night. Will you do that?

CHARLIE I don't know.

DR STRAUSS	If you want to get smart you have to do what I say
CHARLIE	I don't think I'm going to get smart.
DR STRAUSS	Charlie, you don't know it yet, but you're getting smarter all the time. You just won't notice for a while.
CHARLIE	When can I go back to Miss Kinnian's school?
DR STRAUSS	You won't be going back there.
CHARLIE	I want to go back!
DR STRAUSS	Take it easy. Miss Kinnian's going to come to the lab and give you special teaching. It'll be just you and her together. You'll enjoy that, won't you?
CHARLIE	I was mad at her when she didn't come and see me.
DR STRAUSS	She has lots of responsibilities, Charlie. Lots of other people to teach and look after.
CHARLIE	I was really mad.
DR STRAUSS	But you still like her, don't you?
CHARLIE	I like her. Maybe we'll be friends again.
	Out.
CHARLIE	(*tape*): Dr Strauss gave me a present only it wasnt a present but just for lend. I thot it was a little television but it wasnt. He said I got to put it by my bed and turn it on when I go to sleep. I said your kidding why shud I turn it on when Im going to sleep. Who ever herd of a thing like that. But I did it anyway. That stupid TV kept me up all night. How can I sleep with something yelling crazy things all night in my ears. And the stupid pictures.
	I think its crazy. I watch TV all the time and its never made me smart. Maybe you have to sleep while you watch it or it dusnt work.

SCENE 14 *Int: A room at the hospital.*

MISS K	Hello, Charlie.
CHARLIE	Miss Kinnian!
MISS K	How are you?

CHARLIE   I'm tired. Dr Strauss gave me a stupid TV to listen to all night. Only it'll be all right now, because he showed me how to turn the sound right down. He says I don't need to hear it at all.

MISS K   It's called a subconscious learning device.

CHARLIE   That's right! That's what he said. It'll make me smart when I'm asleep. I said what's the point of that? I want to be smart when I'm awake.

MISS K   Good for you, Charlie. What did he say?

CHARLIE   He said it's the same thing. I've got two minds called . . . the *conscious* and the *unconscious*. And they don't talk to each other. That's why I have dreams. I've been having some funny dreams lately. Miss Kinnian?

MISS K   Yes?

CHARLIE   Is it only me, or does everybody have two minds?

Out.

A long moment.

CHARLIE   (*tape*): I've got a headache today. It's from the party. My frends from the factry took me to the pub. I had a good time. I cant wait to be smart like them.

I dont remember how the party was over but I think I went out to buy a newspaper for Joe and Frank and when I came back there was no one their. A nice policeman brot me back home. Thats what my landlady Mrs Flynn says.

Anyway I got a bad headache and Im sick and hurt all over. I dont think Ill drink anymore.

SCENE 15   *Int: The laboratory.*

A beep from the computer and a brief burst of print-out, as before.

BERT   Ready Charlie?

CHARLIE   Ready.

BERT   Go!

A clunk as BERT *trips the mechanism that releases Algernon.*
We hear CHARLIE*'s pencil scraping across the paper.*
Then:

CHARLIE Finished.

CHARLIE *relaxes.*
Then a small buzzer sounds in Algernon's maze.
A moment.

BERT Charlie, you know what?

CHARLIE What?

BERT You won.

CHARLIE *is ecstatic. He can hardly speak.*

CHARLIE Ha! I won! I beat Algernon!

BERT Well done.

CHARLIE I won! I won . . .

He sobers. A moment.

BERT Charlie, what's the matter?

CHARLIE Algernon must feel really bad.

BERT I don't think so.

CHARLIE Course he must. After winning all this time. Poor Algernon.

CHARLIE *is really upset.*

BERT Would you like to hold him?

CHARLIE Can I?

BERT Sure.

CHARLIE Good. It might make him feel better.

BERT *picks up Algernon.*

BERT Here you go.

He hands him over. CHARLIE *is immensely gentle. He hardly dares to breathe.*

CHARLIE He's all soft. Like cotton wool.

BERT Yeah.

CHARLIE And his eyes are black and pink on the edges. He's not so bad. Can I feed him something?

BERT No. He has to earn his food.

CHARLIE What do you mean?

BERT He has to do tests to get it. Like the maze.

CHARLIE Every time? Tests every time?

BERT Sure. Dr Nemur's orders.

CHARLIE I don't think that's right. How would that Dr Nemur like it if he had to pass a test every time he wants to eat? (*Close, quiet*) I think I'll be friends with Algernon.

Out.

SCENE 16 *Int: A room at the hospital.*

CHARLIE *is reading. He is not fully fluent, but is clearly making rapid progress. His stutter is completely gone.*

CHARLIE 'I now began to seriously consider my condition, and I drew up the state of my affairs in writing, not so much to leave them to any that were to come after me, as to deliver my thoughts from daily poring upon them and afflicting my mind.'

MISS K OK, Charlie. We'll stop there for tonight.

CHARLIE Right.

He closes the book and puts it down.
MISS KINNIAN *is a little uneasy.*

MISS K That was good Charlie. Very good.

CHARLIE Don't worry, Miss Kinnian. I'm not smart yet.

MISS K I'm sorry. Forgive me. (*To business*) Are you enjoying the book?

CHARLIE It's very hard. I never read such a hard book before. I feel sorry for him.

MISS K For Robinson Crusoe? Why?

CHARLIE Because he's all alone and has no friends. But I think there must be someone else on that island, because of the picture.

MISS K What picture?

CHARLIE The one on page one hundred and thirty-seven.

Now MISS KINNIAN *is considerably shaken.*

MISS K Just a minute, Charlie.

She picks up the book, leafs through, finds page 137.

Good lord. Go on, Charlie. Tell me about the picture.

CHARLIE The sun's shining and there are birds. He's got his funny umbrella and he's looking at footprints in the sand. So there must be someone there. I hope he gets a friend and not be lonely. Shall I read some more?

MISS K No, not now. Charlie, I want to talk to you.

CHARLIE (*smiling*): You are talking to me.

MISS K Yes . . . Dr Strauss and Dr Nemur let me listen to some of your progress report tapes.

CHARLIE Did you like them?

MISS K They're very good . . . Charlie . . . I think you're a fine person, and I think you're going to show them all.

CHARLIE What will I show them? Who?

MISS KINNIAN *isn't sure if she's doing the right thing.*

MISS K Never mind. No, listen: you shouldn't feel bad if you find out that some people aren't as nice as you think.

CHARLIE What people?

MISS K People you know. At . . . work, maybe.

CHARLIE Oh, you don't need to worry about that. They're smart people. They never do anything that isn't nice. They're my friends.

MISS K Oh Charlie . . .

CHARLIE What's the matter, Miss Kinnian? Have you got something in your eye? Shall I get it out for you?

Out.

CHARLIE *(tape)*: Miss Kinnian said im lerning fast. She looked at me sort of funny. Last night we finished 'Robinson Crusoe'. I want to find out more about what happens to him but Miss Kinnian says thats all there is. Why.

Miss Kinnian teaches me to write better too. Today she told me about commas and all the other things. Punc-tu-a-tion. She showed me how to mix them all up with the words but when I tried she said I did it wrong. I wish I could be smart like her. Shes a genius. She gave me a grammar book so Im going to stop now and read it. Its half passt nine.

Mic bumps and a clunk as he stops the tape.
Silence for a moment.
A burst of tape hiss and room atmosphere as the recording restarts.

CHARLIE *(tape)*: What an idiot I am! I didn't even understand what she was talking about. I read the grammar book last night and it explanes the whole thing. Then I saw it was the same way as Miss Kinnian was trying to tell me, but I just didn't get it. I woke up in the middle of the night, and the whole thing straightened out in my mind.

SCENE 17 *Int:* DR STRAUSS' *room.*

DR STRAUSS *is handling a sheet of paper.*

MISS K I thought you'd want to see.

DR STRAUSS Yes. Thank you. Nemur.

He passes him the paper.

DR NEMUR Show me the previous piece of work again.

MISS K Here, doctor.

He takes it and compares the two sheets.

DR NEMUR Excellent. Excellent. We progress.

Out.

SCENE 18 *Int: A party.*

Loud music. Lots of noise. A burst of laughter.

CHARLIE *is dancing with* ELLEN, *to general amusement.*

JOE   Go on Charlie, get up close to her. You're supposed to be having fun.

FRANK   Watch him Ellen!

CHARLIE   Why isn't anyone else dancing, Ellen?

ELLEN   They're tired. Whoops!

CHARLIE cries out as he falls heavily.
General laughter.

Come on, up you get.

She helps him stand.
He's very unsteady on his feet.

JOE   Getting him up, Ellen?

That gets a dirty laugh.

CHARLIE   Why are they laughing?

ELLEN   Someone told a joke. Come on, Charlie, don't stop, you're the star of the show. Come on.

She tries to force him.

CHARLIE   I don't feel well.

FRANK   Have some more Pepsi.

That gets another laugh.

CHARLIE   It tastes funny.

More laughter.

Why are you laughing? Frank, why are they laughing?

FRANK *laughs in his face.*

Stop it! I don't like it! Stop it!

They close in on him, their baying laughter building.
Eventually, he's trapped in a circle of laughter.
He sways drunkenly.

Let me get by! Please . . .

He stumbles into a side table and knocks it flying.
Stuff goes everywhere. He's almost in tears.

Stop it! Stop it! I want to go home!

Their laughter never stops.

Out.

CHARLIE (*tape*): I felt naked. I wanted to hide myself. I didn't know what to do. Finally, I walked home. It's a funny thing; I never knew that Joe and Frank and the others like to have me around all the time just to make fun of me.

Now I know what it means when they say 'to do a Charlie Gordon.'

I'm ashamed.

SCENE 19 *Int:* CHARLIE*'s room.*

Music. He's listenening to records.
A knock at the door.

CHARLIE Leave me alone.

MRS FLYNN (*outside*): Charlie? Charlie let me in.

CHARLIE I don't want to.

A moment. Then the door opens.

I didn't say you could come in!

MRS FLYNN (*at the door*): I'm sorry, Charlie.

CHARLIE What do you want, Mrs Flynn?

MRS FLYNN (*approaching tentatively*): I wanted to see if you're all right. Are you sick?

CHARLIE (*seizing on the idea*): Yes! Yes, I am. I'm ill.

MRS FLYNN You don't look ill.

CHARLIE I'd like you to phone the factory for me and tell them I'm ill. Please do that.

MRS FLYNN Shall I call a doctor?

CHARLIE That won't be necessary. Just the factory. Will you do it?

MRS FLYNN I don't know, Charlie . . .

CHARLIE (*an order*): Please do it!

A frozen moment. MRS FLYNN *is a little scared of him.*

MRS FLYNN (*backing off*): Yes . . . Yes, of course, Charlie.

Whatever you say. Whatever you say.

She fumbles her way out of the door.
She shuts it behind her.
CHARLIE *'s breathing is tense and nervy.*
He turns off the music, then slams a tape into his
portable recorder and switches it to record.
He takes a moment to compose his thoughts.

CHARLIE I think it's a good thing about finding out how everybody laughs at me. I thought about it a lot. It's because I'm so stupid I don't even know when I'm doing something stupid. People think it's funny when a retarded person can't do things the same way they can.

Anyway, now I know I'm getting smarter every day. I know punctuation and I can spell good. There are times when I can close my eyes and think of a page and it all comes back like a picture.

Besides history, geography, and arithmetic, Miss Kinnian said I should now start to learn a few foreign languages. Dr Strauss gave me some more tapes to play while I sleep. I still don't understand how that conscious and unconscious mind works, but Dr Strauss says not to worry yet.

When I become intelligent like Dr Strauss says, with three times my IQ of 68, then maybe I'll be like everyone else and people will like me and be friendly.

Dr Nemur says I have to take a Rorshach test tomorrow. (*Wearily*) I wonder what *that* is?

He switches off the machine.
Out.

SCENE 20 *Int: Another room.*

BERT *the technician sorts out his cards, as before.*

BERT OK, Charlie, here we go.

CHARLIE It's the inkblot test!

BERT Sorry?

CHARLIE   The cards with the inkblots on them. I took this test
           before. Before the operation.

BERT   Ah, you remember, do you?

CHARLIE   (*angrily*): Of course I remember.

BERT   Yes, of course. Sorry.

CHARLIE   Right.

BERT   OK. Now, I want you to look at this first card . . .

           He lays a card on the table.

           What might this be? People see all sorts of things in
           these inkblots. Tell me what it might be for you.
           What does it make you think of?

CHARLIE   (*amazed*): What did you say?

BERT   What does it make you think of?

CHARLIE   You mean there are no pictures hidden in those
           inkblots?

BERT   What?

CHARLIE   Pictures. Hidden in the inkblots. Last time you told
           me that everyone could see them and you wanted
           me to find them too.

BERT   Charlie, last time I used almost exactly the same
           words I used just now. I always say the same thing.

CHARLIE   I don't believe you.

BERT   Why should I lie?

CHARLIE   To make fun of me.

BERT   Charlie!

CHARLIE   I was sure . . .

           CHARLIE *is very uncertain. He pulls himself together.*

           Show me that card.

           He slides it towards himself.

           It looks like a pair of bats hanging upside down.
           Next.

           BERT *puts down another.*

           Two men fencing. Next.

The speed builds.

A clown's face. A vase of flowers. A lion. A butterfly with an injured wing. Wait.

BERT What?

CHARLIE How can you be sure I'm not just saying anything at random? How do you know I'm not making a fool of you?

Out.

CHARLIE (*tape*): I went back to the factory. I figured out a new way to line up the machines on the production line, and I overheard Mr Donnegan the owner say it will save thousands of pounds a year in labour and increased production. He gave me a fifty pound bonus. Tomorrow I plan to take Joe and Frank out to lunch to celebrate.

SCENE 21 *Int: The factory floor.*

JOE *and* FRANK *are very uneasy with the new* CHARLIE.

JOE No, sorry, Charlie mate. I've got to do some shopping for the wife. I promised, you know?

FRANK Yeah, and I'm meeting my cousin for lunch. Arranged it weeks ago. Bleeding shame.

JOE Yeah. (*Escaping*) Sorry.

FRANK (*going*): Yeah . . .

A moment. CHARLIE *sighs, dunks his mop in its bucket and drains it off.*
Out.

CHARLIE (*tape*): It's almost as if they're afraid of me. Hardly anybody talks to me, or jokes around the way they used to. It makes the job sort of lonely. I'm going to try to get up the nerve to ask Miss Kinnian to have dinner with me to celebrate my bonus. I'll ask her tonight at the hospital.

SCENE 22 *Int: DR STRAUSS' room.*

A fierce argument is in progress.

DR NEMUR For God's sake, Strauss! It's my experiment and my research, and I'll publish the results whenever I think fit.

DR STRAUSS Your experiment? Who performed the operation? Whose techniques made the whole thing possible? Who found him, for God's sake?

DR NEMUR Joint names then, I'll grant you that.

DR STRAUSS Oh, thank you very much.

DR NEMUR But we publish at the end of this month.

DR STRAUSS It's too soon! We're still not one hundred percent sure.

DR NEMUR Too soon. If we wait any longer, word will get out anyway.

DR STRAUSS And spoil your thunder!

As the argument continues, we cut to:

SCENE 23 *Int: Outside the door.*

Very close, CHARLIE *is listening to the muffled voices. We hear him wincing at the ferocity of the row.*

DR NEMUR What do you mean by that?

DR STRAUSS You're more interested in your own glory than you are in the experiment. Charlie means nothing to you.

DR NEMUR My glory! What about you? You're just trying to ride to fame on my work.

DR STRAUSS Your work would mean nothing without my breakthrough in neurosurgery.

DR NEMUR Breakthrough! You flatter yourself, doctor . . .

But all this has been going on behind:

MISS K (*Off*) Charlie?

CHARLIE *jumps.*

CHARLIE Miss Kinnian.

MISS K (*approaching*): Why are you waiting out here?

CHARLIE They're arguing again. Come away.

He leads her down the corridor.
We go with them. The argument fades.

They argue all the time now.

MISS K Yes, I know.

CHARLIE Miss Kinnian . . .

MISS K Yes, Charlie?

CHARLIE I have something to ask you . . .

Out.

CHARLIE (*tape*): I don't understand why I never noticed how beautiful Miss Kinnian really is. She has brown eyes and feathery brown hair that comes to the top of her neck. She's only thirty-four! I think from the beginning I had the feeling that she was an unreachable genius – and very, very old. Now, every time I see her she grows younger and more lovely.

SCENE 24 *Int: A restaurant.*

Quiet and elegant. Very muted music plays.
CHARLIE *pours some wine.*

CHARLIE There.

MISS K Thank you.

They drink. A moment.

You know, Charlie, you'll soon be leaving me behind.

CHARLIE (*laughingly*): Hardly.

MISS K It's true. You're already a better reader than I am. You can take in a whole page at a glance. And you remember every single word you read.

CHARLIE I don't feel intelligent. There are so many things I don't understand.

MISS K You've got to be patient. You're accomplishing in weeks what takes normal people half a lifetime. It's amazing. You're like a giant sponge, soaking things in. Facts, figures, general knowledge. And soon you'll begin to connect them.

CHARLIE Connect them?

MISS K All the different branches of learning are related. They're like steps on a giant ladder that take you up higher and higher to see more and more of the world around you.

CHARLIE That's a wonderful way of putting it.

MISS K I can see only a little bit of the whole, Charlie, and I won't go much higher than I am now – but you'll keep climbing up and up, and see more and more, and each step will open new worlds that you never even knew existed. (*A moment*) I hope . . . I just hope to God –

CHARLIE What?

MISS K I just hope I wasn't wrong, advising you to go into this in the first place.

CHARLIE (*laughingly*): How could you be? It worked, didn't it?

MISS K (*not reassured*): Yes, it worked.

A moment. They look at each other.

CHARLIE I know what you're thinking. No guarantee of permanence. Cheer up. Algernon is still smart, isn't he? And this is only the beginning for me. I know it.

Out.

CHARLIE (*tape*): No guarantee of permanence. I didn't want to think of what that might mean, any more than elderly people want to think about death. But I hadn't lied to her. And I understood what she meant about the levels, because I'd seen some of them already. The thought of leaving her behind made me sad.

I'm in love with Miss Kinnian.

SCENE 25 *Int:* DONNEGAN*'s office.*

A secretary types in an outer room.

MR D Close the door, Charlie.

CHARLIE does so. The typing continues, muted. DONNEGAN is ill at ease.

Look, Charlie . . .

He tails off.

CHARLIE What can I do for you, Mr Donnegan?

MR D I want you to look at this.

He hands CHARLIE *a thin sheaf of papers.* CHARLIE *scans it briefly, riffling the sheets.*

It's a petition.

CHARLIE Yes, I can see that.

MR D Everybody on the factory floor signed it. All hundred and fifty of them.

CHARLIE Except Mary Carter.

MR D What?

CHARLIE Mary Carter, Mrs Carter, in packing. Her name isn't on this list. She's the only one.

MR D Jesus.

CHARLIE And everyone else demands that you fire me.

MR D What's happened to you – they don't think it's right.

CHARLIE (*quite sharply*): How can you say that? What's wrong with a man becoming intelligent?

A moment. DONNEGAN *has no answer to that.*

MR D I think it would be best for all concerned if you left.

CHARLIE So you are going to fire me.

MR D I was hoping you'd leave of your own free will. It'd be less . . .

CHARLIE Embarrassing? (*A moment*) Will you tell me something?

MR D What?

CHARLIE Before, when they laughed at me, they despised me for my ignorance; now, they hate me for my knowledge. What in God's name do they want of me?

Out.

CHARLIE (*tape*): This is the first tape I've recorded since I left the factory. Just over two weeks ago. Dr Strauss is very angry at me for not doing more progress reports. And he's justified, because the hospital is now paying me a regular salary. I told him I was too busy thinking and reading, and showed him some notes I'd typed up. He reminded me yet again about the need to speak and write simply so that people will be able to understand me.

Dr Strauss and Dr Nemur reached an agreement about publishing their work and their findings. They're going to present Algernon and myself to the annual conference of the World Psychological Association next Tuesday.

Prolonged loud applause from the conference audience. It mixes down to:

SCENE 26 *Int: A reception room.*

A select party in progress.

DR STRAUSS Well, Charlie. We created quite a sensation.

CHARLIE So it seems.

DR NEMUR We're very proud of you, Charlie, very proud.

CHARLIE And of Algernon?

They laugh uneasily, not sure if he's joking.

DR STRAUSS Of course. Of course.

CHARLIE Good. 'Charlie and Algernon', 'Algernon and Charlie' – two interchangeable experimental animals. We should be treated alike.

DR STRAUSS Please, Charlie.

CHARLIE What a shame you couldn't get Algernon to make a few tapes before his operation. You might have raised even more laughs than you did with mine.

They don't know what to say.

PROF S (*approaching*): Strauss! Nemur! What are you doing skulking over here all by yourselves? People want to meet you.

CHARLIE   Good afternoon, Professor Sherrinford.

PROF S   Good afternoon to you. Well, Nemur – that was a very impressive presentation.

DR NEMUR   Thank you, David.

PROF S   Brilliant work, the pair of you. And what do you think of these two geniuses then, Charlie?

CHARLIE   Well, David.

SHERRINFORD *laughs uneasily at this barb.*

My first impression of Dr Nemur was that he was indeed a genius.

NEMUR *shrugs this off.*
SHERRINFORD is *somewhat embarrassed. He didn't expect to prompt a serious answer.*

But now I realise that although he has a very good mind, he's shackled by self-doubt. That's why it's so important for him to feel that his work is accepted by the world.

DR NEMUR   I hardly think – (*that is the case* . . .)

CHARLIE   Dr Strauss on the other hand might be called a genius, although I feel that his areas of knowledge are too limited – presumably due to his being educated in the tradition of narrow specialisation.

DR STRAUSS   That's an extremely sweeping statement, Charlie.

CHARLIE   Is it? I was shocked when you told me that the only ancient languages you can read are Latin, Greek, and Hebrew. And you know almost nothing of mathematics beyond the elementary levels of the calculus of variations.

PROF S   And this shocked you, Mr Gordon?

CHARLIE   More than shocked, Professor. When I first discovered it, I was almost . . . angered.

PROF S   Angered. Fascinating.

CHARLIE   It was as if he'd been hiding the truth in order to deceive me. Pretending to be what he is not. (*A moment*) No one I've ever known is what he appears to be on the surface.

Out.

CHARLIE (*tape*): Dr Nemur has stopped our regular analysis sessions. He's increasingly uncomfortable around me. Sometimes when I try to talk to him, he just looks at me strangely and turns away. I was angry at first when Dr Strauss told me I was giving Dr Nemur an inferiority complex. I thought he was mocking me and I'm over-sensitive at being made fun of.

How was I to know that a highly respected psycho-experimentalist like Nemur was unacquainted with Hindustani and Chinese? I asked Dr Strauss how Nemur could refute Rahajamati's attack on his method and results if Nemur couldn't even read them in the first place. That strange look on Dr Strauss' face could only mean one of two things. Either he doesn't want to tell Nemur what they're saying in India, or else – and this worries me – Dr Strauss doesn't know either.

I must be careful to speak and write clearly and simply so that people won't laugh.

SCENE 27 *Int: A classroom.*

MISS KINNIAN *is teaching her class of slow adults. One man reads laboriously.*

MAN The boy runs down the street. See him run. His friends run after him. See them run and laugh.

MISS K Very good, Robert.

MAN Thank you, Miss Kinnian.

MISS K OK everyone, it's time to go home now.

The students begin to leave.
Several 'Goodbye Miss Kinnian's.

Goodbye Audrey, goodbye Malcolm. See you all next week. Don't forget your books. Bye.

The classroom empties.
MISS KINNIAN *begins to gather up the stuff from her desk. Suddenly*

CHARLIE *(at the door)*: Good evening, Miss Kinnian.

He has startled her. And she is still not sure of how to behave with him.

MISS K Charlie! Good evening.

CHARLIE May I come in?

MISS K Of course.

CHARLIE *(approaching)*: Thank you.

MISS K How are you? How was the conference?

CHARLIE I should have been prepared for it. I knew I was going to be on display. But even so . . .

MISS K What? Prepared for what?

CHARLIE Nemur seems to think that he hasn't so much helped me as created me. That if it wasn't for him I wouldn't exist at all. I knew he saw me as less than human before, but it came as a shock to realise that nothing's chai China by CTPS m just a test result.

His outburst hangs in the air.
An awkward moment.

MISS K Charlie, why did you come here?

CHARLIE I haven't seen you for over a week.

MISS K There's nothing I can teach you any more. You must know that.

CHARLIE I wanted you to talk to me, not teach me. Have you had dinner?

MISS K Yes. I have.

CHARLIE Then may I buy you a drink?

MISS K I have my car here . . . I shouldn't . . .

CHARLIE Coffee then.

Out.

SCENE 28 *Int: A cafe-cum-sandwich-bar.*

Quietly busy. CHARLIE*'s mood is much lighter.*

CHARLIE But it's so wonderfully simple! It has true elegance. The last movement of the fifth concerto is a perfect

example of the mathematical variance equivalent
applied to an everyday construct.

MISS K (*laughing, good-naturedly*): Charlie, stop!

CHARLIE (*shocked, angry*): Miss Kinnian!

MISS K (*instantly serious*): Forgive me. I wasn't laughing at
you.

CHARLIE (*not convinced*): No?

MISS K No. Certainly not.

But she cannot convince him. A moment.

CHARLIE I can't communicate with anyone very much, now.

MISS K Oh Charlie . . .

CHARLIE I must read Vrostadt's equations again.

MISS K Vrostadt?

CHARLIE 'Levels of Semantic Progression'. It's brilliant, but
there's so much more he could have covered . . .
Thank God for my books and my music . . .

A sudden crash as someone drops a pile of plates.
MISS KINNIAN *jumps.*
The other customers react jeeringly:

CUSTOMER Good catch!/Nice one!/Well, *he* didn't work here
long!/Want some more?

*The plates were dropped by a rather slow-witted young
man. He is confused and scared by the comments.*

BOY I didn't do it on purpose.

This gets a laugh.

I didn't!

OWNER (*approaching*): All right, don't just stand there.
Clean up this mess.

BOY Right.

OWNER Not like that, you idiot!

The boy cringes.

(*Softer*): Not with your hands. You'll cut yourself.
Get the broom.

BOY	The broom?
OWNER	The broom from the kitchen.
BOY	(*no longer scared*): The broom. Right!
CUSTOMER	He's not so stupid – it's easier to break 'em than wash 'em up.

Big laugh.

BOY	(*slowly getting the joke*): Yes! Yes!

He laughs happily.
We suddenly become aware of CHARLIE, *close to mic, chuckling warmly.*

MISS K	(*low, shocked*): Charlie!
CHARLIE	(*absently, still smiling*): What?

Then he realises what he's doing.
His smile freezes. He's very shaken.

My God . . .

Out.

SCENE 29 *Ext: A street. Night.*

CHARLIE	I was laughing at him. Just like all those others. *Me*!
MISS K	But you stopped.
CHARLIE	Did you see his reaction? He joined in. He thought they were being friendly. He liked it!
MISS K	(*gently*): It's a very common reaction. I know it's upsetting, but . . .
CHARLIE	And I'd almost forgotten . . .
MISS K	Forgotten what?
CHARLIE	That was me in there! The Charlie Gordon I used to be.
MISS K	Charlie . . .
CHARLIE	No! No, I didn't forget . . . You can't forget what you've never known . . .
MISS K	I don't understand.
CHARLIE	I never really knew what I was like. Back then, I wasn't capable of understanding it – oh, I knew that

I was inferior, that everyone else had something that had been denied to me, but that was all I knew. And later, I just blocked it out, refused to think about it. And now . . . it took that simple-minded boy to make me see the truth.

Out.

CHARLIE (*tape*): This day was good for me. Seeing the past more clearly, I have decided to use my knowledge and skills to work in the field of increasing human intelligence levels. Who is better equipped for this work? Who else has lived in both worlds? These are my people. Let me use my gift to do something for them.

SCENE 30 *Int:* DR STRAUSS' *room.*

DR STRAUSS What exactly do you have in mind?

CHARLIE The calculus of intelligence. Mathematical research backed up by practical experimentation.

DR NEMUR On yourself?

CHARLIE Can you think of a more appropriate subject? But on the test animals too. I'll need a lab of my own and designated computer time. I can work at nights – that will make it easier to timetable.

DR STRAUSS I'll see what can be arranged.

CHARLIE Dr Strauss, I have to do this.

DR NEMUR I have several reservations . . .

CHARLIE Nemur, I'll be working *with* you, not in competition. I admire your work too much to want to take it from you. You must understand that. There's so much that might be done! If I could be made into a genius, what might be achieved by using this technique on normal people? Or on *geniuses*?

Out.

SCENE 31 *Int: The lab.*

BERT Charlie! Hello. Haven't seen you down here lately.

CHARLIE I've been busy. How's Algernon?

BERT   He's a bit uppity today. Didn't feel like working for his breakfast.

CHARLIE   I told you that was wrong. He obviously agrees with me.

BERT   Well let's see if he'd like some lunch.

He sets up the test-box with several sliding latches.

There we go . . . Would you bring him over, Charlie?

CHARLIE   Sure . . . (*Moving off*) Hello, Algernon. What's all this about a hunger-strike then?

CHARLIE *unlatches Algernon's small metal cage.*

Come on with you . . .

He suddenly cries out in surprise.

BERT   What?

CHARLIE *slams the cage door shut.*
A moment.

CHARLIE   He bit me.

Out.

CHARLIE   (*tape*): Algernon is changing. He's less co-operative, and has to be fed every meal. They're all pretending that his character changes aren't necessarily significant for me. But it's hard to ignore the fact that some of the other animals who were used in this experiment are also showing strange behaviour.

I'm going ahead with my plans to carry the Strauss–Nemur research forward. With all due respect to both of them, I'm well aware of their limitations. If there is a reason for the aberrant behaviour, I'll have to find it out for myself.

SCENE 32   *Int:* CHARLIE's *lab.*

He is working at a computer terminal, entering data with enormous speed and dexterity.
A knock at the door.
CHARLIE *doesn't stop typing.*

CHARLIE   One moment.

He presses a final key. The computer beeps.
A burst of rapid print-out.
CHARLIE *relaxes and stretches.*

Come in.

The door opens.

DR STRAUSS Charlie.

CHARLIE Dr Strauss.

DR STRAUSS How long have you been working?

CHARLIE What's the time?

DR STRAUSS Eleven twenty.

CHARLIE A.M.?

DR STRAUSS Charlie, you won't find *me* here at eleven twenty at night.

CHARLIE You think I'm working too hard.

DR STRAUSS I think you should at least take the occasional rest. And sleep the odd night in your own bed and not on that contraption.

CHARLIE It's surprisingly comfortable once you get used to it . . . You're right, of course.

DR STRAUSS Of course.

CHARLIE But I can't stop. Not until I know.

DR STRAUSS And when will that be?

CHARLIE Soon. It has to be soon.

Out.

SCENE 33 *Int:* DR STRAUSS*' room.*

NEMUR *is handling a manuscript.*

DR NEMUR (*reads*): 'The Algernon–Gordon Effect'.

CHARLIE I suppose I've taken a liberty given it that name.

DR NEMUR 'A study of the structure and function of increased intelligence'.

DR STRAUSS Charlie, you can't produce a final report after only five days' work.

CHARLIE But there's no more to be done. I'd like you both to

read it and arrange for publication. The maths ought
to be checked.

DR STRAUSS By whom? I doubt if either of us . . .

He trails off.

CHARLIE I've checked and rechecked my results a dozen
times. I hoped I was in error.

DR NEMUR What are you saying?

CHARLIE You'll understand when you read the report. I'm
only sorry that my own contribution to the field has
to rest on the ashes of your work.

DR STRAUSS The ashes? You believe our technique has no future?

CHARLIE It's not a question of belief. I *know*. The increase of
human intelligence by surgical means has no
practical application whatsoever. I'm truly sorry.

Out.

CHARLIE (*tape*): The hypothesis proven in my report can be
described quite simply: artificially increased
intelligence deteriorates at a rate of time directly
proportional to the quantity of the increase.
Inherent flaws in the technique mean that lasting
stability is quite unattainable.

It's now certain that Algernon has regressed
mentally. Motor activity is impaired and there's an
accelerated loss of co-ordination. There's also a
strong indication of progressive amnesia. These and
other physical deterioration syndromes can all be
predicted by the formulae in my report.

Although my findings are irrefutable, I plan to
continue with my research. I tell myself that this is
not in itself a symptom of irrationality.

SCENE 34 *Int:* CHARLIE *'s lab.*

A burst of print-out.
As it stops, CHARLIE *tears the paper from the machine
and reads it.*
He is impatient and short-tempered.
A knock at the door.

CHARLIE (*very curtly*): What?

The door opens.

DR NEMUR Excuse me Charlie . . .

CHARLIE What? What do you want?

A moment as NEMUR *takes in the change in him.*

DR NEMUR There is something you should see.

CHARLIE Nemur, this is important.

DR NEMUR So is this.

Out.

SCENE 35 *Int: The test lab.*

Algernon is dead.
CHARLIE *has been shocked out of his anger, and
everyone is very wary of what this new development
might mean.*

CHARLIE When did it happen?

BERT He was dead when I came in this morning.

CHARLIE You'll dissect, of course.

DR STRAUSS I must examine the brain. If there are physical
changes . . .

CHARLIE Of course. You'll get a copy of the results to me?

DR NEMUR As soon as we can.

CHARLIE Thank you (*A moment*) When you've finished with
him . . .

DR STRAUSS Yes, Charlie?

CHARLIE I'd like to bury him. Somewhere nice.

Out.

CHARLIE (*tape*): It's definite. We now have physical
corroboration of the theoretical prediction. Algernon's
brain had become lighter and there was a smoothing
out of the cerebral convolutions. Now that I know, I
don't want it to happen to me. I put his body in a
shoe box and buried it in my back yard.

I cried.

SCENE 36   *Int: The landing outside* CHARLIE*'s room.*

DR STRAUSS *knocks on the door.*

DR STRAUSS   Charlie? Charlie, come on.

He knocks again. No response.

You're sure he's in there?

MRS FLYNN   Oh yes.

DR STRAUSS   He's not been in to the lab for five days.

MRS FLYNN   He's not been anywhere.

STRAUSS *knocks again.*

DR STRAUSS   Charlie!

Abruptly, the door opens.

CHARLIE   Leave me alone!

MRS FLYNN   But Charlie – *we're worried* . . .

CHARLIE   I w-want you to l-leave me alone! G-go away!

This is the first time his stutter has come back. CHARLIE *is horrified. A moment of his frantic gasping for breath, then he slams the door and locks it.*
Out.
A long moment.

CHARLIE   (*tape*): I feel the darkness closing in. It's hard to throw off thoughts of suicide. I keep telling myself how important this introspective recorded journal will be.

Today, I picked up 'Paradise Lost'. I remembered how great I thought John Milton was, but when I opened the book I couldn't understand it at all. I got so angry I threw it across the room.

I've got to try to hold on to some of it. Some of the things I've learned. Oh God, please don't take it all away.

SCENE 37   *Ext: A street. Night.*

Pouring with rain. Traffic roars past, throwing up spray.

POLICEMAN   Are you all right, sir?

CHARLIE   Yes, constable, yes, I'm fine. Thank you . . .

But he doesn't sound it.

POLICEMAN   Bit of a wet night for a stroll, isn't it?

CHARLIE   Yes. Yes, I suppose it is.

POLICEMAN   Far to go, have you, sir?

CHARLIE   I beg your pardon?

POLICEMAN   Where do you live?

The question distresses CHARLIE.

CHARLIE   Well . . .

POLICEMAN   Come on, it's a simple enough question. Where do you live?

And CHARLIE*'s last shred of control snaps:*

CHARLIE   I can't remember! . . . I can't remember.

Out.

CHARLIE   (*tape*): I've got to fight it. I won't let it happen. The amnesia isn't constant. I lie in bed for days and I don't know who or where I am, but then it all comes back to me in a flash. I can't help thinking of the boy in the cafe, the blank expression, the silly smile, the people laughing at him . . .

He pulls himself together with an effort.

I must be analytical. I'm forgetting things that I learned recently. It seems to be following the classic pattern – the last things learned are the first things forgotten. Or is that the pattern? I'd better look it up again . . .

SCENE 38   *Int*: CHARLIE*'s lab.*

He is furtively – and clumsily – gathering papers and books.
He drops something and curses under his breath.
As he gathers the dropped stuff, the door opens. A frozen moment.

DR NEMUR   (*in the doorway*): Hello, Charlie.

CHARLIE   I hoped I could do this without anyone seeing.

DR NEMUR   (*approaching*): What have you got there?

CHARLIE   Some of my research material. I want to check a few things.

DR NEMUR   Of course. Dr Strauss and I have been very worried about you.

CHARLIE   He keeps coming round to my room. But I don't let him in.

DR NEMUR   I know. Why don't you let him in, Charlie?

CHARLIE   I just want to be left alone. It's important that I record the . . . the changes.

DR NEMUR   Couldn't you do that here? We could help you.

CHARLIE   I don't want your help! (*Calmer*) I can manage. I needed some more material, that's all.

DR NEMUR   (*coming very close*): May I see?

He gently takes a report from CHARLIE.

'Uber psychische Ganzheit'. Did you find this useful?

CHARLIE   What did you say?

DR NEMUR   Uber psychische Ganzheit.

CHARLIE   (*very shaken*): Give me that!

He drops everything else he's holding and snatches the report.
Frantically, he leafs through the slim volume.

(*Scarcely audible*): Oh no. No . . .

Out.

CHARLIE   (*tape*): At first I thought there was something wrong with my eyes. Then I realised. I couldn't read German anymore. I tested myself in other languages. All gone.

That was last Tuesday. And since then . . . Most of the books I have here are too hard for me now. I get angry with them. I keep telling myself I must keep going with these reports, so that someone will know what's happening to me. But it's getting harder and harder. I couldn't bring myself to tape

anything until today. It's Sunday today. I know
because I can see through my window people
going to church. I think I stayed in bed all week,
but I'm not sure.

I think of my mother and father a lot these days. I
found a picture of them with me. My father has a
big ball under his arm. He never shaved much and
he used to scratch my face when he hugged me. He
said he was going to take me to see cows on a farm
once but he never did.

SCENE 39 *Int:* CHARLIE*'s room.*

He is asleep, breathing fitfully.

MISS K (*close, gentle*): Charlie? Charlie?

He stirs, uneasily.

Charlie, wake up.

He slowly surfaces, then reacts with horror.

CHARLIE Miss Kinnian! Go away!

He cowers under the sheets.

MISS K Don't be frightened, Charlie.

CHARLIE I don't want to see you. (*A sudden thought*) How
did you get in?

MISS K The door wasn't locked.

CHARLIE *throws back the sheets and stands.*
He grabs her roughly.

Charlie! Let go of me. What are you doing?

He pushes her towards the door.

CHARLIE I want you to go away.

MISS K Charlie, you're hurting me.

CHARLIE You shouldn't have come in. You shouldn't have
seen me.

MISS K But Charlie . . .

CHARLIE Go away!

*With a grunt of effort he pushes her out of the open
door. He slams it shut and locks it. She hammers on*

it, close to tears.

MISS K   Let me in! I want to help you!

CHARLIE   You can't help me.

MISS K   Charlie. Please . . .

CHARLIE *is also close to crying.*

CHARLIE   Go away! (*A moment*) I don't like you any more!
Out.

CHARLIE   (*tape*): It wasnt true what I said to Miss Kinnian. I
said I didnt like her no more, but its not true. I still
love her. But I didnt let her in because I didnt want
her to laugh at me like I remember her doing
before. She gave Mrs Flynn money to pay my rent. I
think I lost this months money from the hospital but
I dont remember. Mrs Flynn said the way I just lie
around all the time reminds her of her son before
she threw him out. She said am I sick cause if im
sick thats one thing but if im a loafer thats another
thing and she wont have it, I told her I think im
sick.

Its sunday again. I dont have anything to do
because my tv set is broke. I tryd to read some
stories but I have to read the same bit over and over
again because I dont know what they mean.

Please dont let me forget how to read altogether.

A long silence.
A clunk. The tape resumes, but time has passed.
CHARLIE *has deteriorated further.*

CHARLIE   (*tape*): Its wensdy. I think its wensdy. Mrs Flynn
called a strange doctor to see me. She was afraid I
was going to die. I told the doctor I wasnt too sick
and that I only forget sometimes. He asked me did I
have any friends or relatives and I said no I dont
have any. I told him I had a friend called Algernon
once but he was a mouse and we used to run races
together. He looked at me funny like he thought I
was crazy.

He smiled when I told him I used to be a genius.
He talked to me like I was a baby and he winked at
Mrs Flynn. I got mad and chased him out because
he was making fun of me the way they all used to.

I put sum flowers on Algernons grave today. Mrs
Flynn thinks Im stupid to put flowers on a mouses
grave but I told her algernon was special.

Mrs Flynn says Ive got to pay the rent because I
havent paid for over two months.

SCENE 40   *Int: The factory floor.*

CHARLIE *wrings out his mop and starts mopping the
floor.*

MAN 2   (*off*): Hey, you!

CHARLIE   Me?

MAN 2   (*approaching*): You see anyone else?

CHARLIE   (*looking round*): Lots of people.

MAN 2   Well I'm talking to you. So, you're the famous
Charlie Gordon.

CHARLIE   Hello.

MAN 2   They say you're a real mastermind.

CHARLIE   No . . .

MAN 2   Say something clever.

CHARLIE   I've got to clean the floor . . .

MAN 2   Go on – say something intelligent.

He is grabbed from behind by JOE.

Hey!

JOE   Leave him alone.

CHARLIE   Joe!

JOE   Hello Charlie. We heard you was back.

FRANK   Hi Charlie.

CHARLIE   Hello Frank.

MAN 2   Let go of me!

FRANK   When you've learnt your lesson. Lay off him, right?

MAN 2   I was just having a joke, for God's sake.

JOE   Well perhaps he don't think it's funny.

MAN 2   He wouldn't know a joke if you hit him in the bloody face with it. Bloody dumbo.

He winces as JOE'S *grip tightens.*

JOE   He's got more guts than you'll ever have. So knock it off. Right?

MAN 2   Alright!

FRANK   Good. Now get lost.

JOE *pushes the man away.*

MAN 2   (*going*): Just a joke. Christ . . .

JOE   Charlie, listen. If anbody bothers you, you call me or Frank, right?

CHARLIE   (*very moved*): Right. Thank you Joe. Right.

Out.

CHARLIE   (*tape*): Its good to have friends. Its good.

After work I did a stupid thing. I forgot I wasnt in Miss Kinnians class at the night scool any more like I use to be. I went in and sat down in my old seat in the back of the room and she looked at me funny and she said Charles. I dint remember she ever called me that before only Charlie so I said hello Miss Kinnian Im redy for my lesin today only I lost my book that we was using. She startid to cry and run out of the room and everybody looked at me and I saw they wasnt the same pepul who used to be in my class.

Then all of a sudden I remember some things about the operashun and me getting smart and I said golly I reely done a Charlie Gordon that time. I went away before she come back to the room. Thats why Im going away from here for good. I dont want to do nothing like that agen. I dont want Miss Kinnian to feel sorry for me. Evry body feels sorry for me at the factery and I dont want that eather so Im going somewhere where nobody knows that Charlie Gordon was once a genius and now he cant even reed a book or rite good.

Im taking a cuple of books along with me and even if I cant reed them Ill practise hard and maybe I wont forget every thing I lerned. If I try reel hard maybe Ill be a littel bit smarter then I was before the operashun. I got my rabits foot and my luky penny and maybe they will help me.

If you ever hear this Miss Kinnian dont be sorry for me. Im glad I got a second chanse to be smart because I lerned a lot of things that I never even new were in this world and Im grateful that I saw it all for a little bit. I dont know why Im stupid agen or what I did wrong maybe its becaus I dint try hard enuff.

Good-by Miss Kinnian and Dr Strauss and evrybody.

A moment. The tape hisses on.

Please tell Dr Nemur not to be so upset when pepul laff at him and he would have more friends. Its easy to make frends if you let pepul laff at you. Im going to have lots of frends where I go.

A long silence. Finally:

Please if you get a chanse put some flowrs on Algernons grave in the bak yard.

He has finished. But the tape still runs.
He's forgotten to turn it off.
We listen for a long moment to the room atmosphere and the tape hiss.
Then it's overtaken by music.
Closing announcements.
The music ends.

The end.

SHORT STORY

progris riport 1 – martch 5 1965

Dr Strauss says I shud rite down what I think and evrey thing
that happins to me from now on. I dont know why but he says
its importint so they will see if they will use me. I hope they
use me. Miss Kinnian says maybe they can make me smart. I
want to be smart. My name is Charlie Gordon. I am 37 years
old and 2 weeks ago was my birthday. I have nuthing more to
rite now so I will close for today.

progris riport 2 – martch 6

I had a test today. I think I faled it. and I think that may be
now they wont use me. What happind is a nice young man was
in the room and he had some white cards with ink spilled all
over them. He sed Charlie what do you see on this card. I was
very skared even tho I had my rabits foot in my pockit because
when I was a kid I always faled tests in school and I spilled ink
to.

I told him I saw a inkblot. He said yes and it made me feel
good. I thot that was all but when I got up to go he stopped
me. He said now sit down Charlie we are not thru yet. Then I
don't remember so good but he wantid me to say what was in
the ink. I dint see nuthing in the ink but he said there was
picturs there other pepul saw some picturs. I coudnt see any
picturs. I reely tryed to see. I held the card close up and then
far away. Then I said if I had my glases I coud see better I
usally only ware my glases in the movies or TV but I said they
are in the closit in the hall. I got them. Then I said let me see
that card agen I bet Ill find it now.

I tryed hard but I still coudnt find the picturs I only saw the
ink. I told him may be I need new glases. He rote somthing
down on a paper and I got skared of faling the test. I told him
it was a very nice inkblot with littel points all around the edges.
He looked very sad so that wasnt it. I said please let me try
agen. Ill get it in a few minits becaus Im not so fast somtimes.
Im a slow reeder too in Miss Kinnians class for slow adults but
Im trying very hard.

He gave me a chance with another card that had 2 kinds of
ink spilled on it red and blue.

He was very nice and talked slow like Miss Kinnian does
and he explaned it to me that it was a *raw shok*. He said pepul
see things in the ink. I said show me where. He said think. I
told him I think a inkblot but that wasn't rite eather. He said
what does it remind you – pretend something. I closd my eyes
for a long time to pretend. I told him I pretned a fowntan pen
with ink leeking all over a table cloth. Then he got up and
went out.

I dont think I passd the *raw shok* test.

progris report 3 – martch 7

Dr Strauss and Dr Nemur say it dont matter about the inkblots.
I told them I dint spill the ink on the cards and I coudn't see
anything in the ink. They said that maybe they will still use me.
I said Miss Kinnian never gave me tests like that one only
spellin and reading. They said Miss Kinnian told that I was her
bestist pupil in the adult nite scool becaus I tryed the hardist
and I reely wantid to lern. They said how come you went to
the adult nite scool all by yourself Charlie. How did you find it.
I said I askd pepul and sumbldy told me where I shud go to
lern to read and spell good. They said why did you want to. I
told them becaus all my life I wantid to be smart and not
dumb. But its very hard to be smart. They said you know it will
probly be tempirery. I said yes. Miss Kinnian told me. I dont
care if it herts.

Later I had more crazy tests today. The nice lady who gave it
me told me the name and I asked her how do you spellit so I
can rite it in my progris riport. THEMATIC APPERCEPTION TEST. I
dont know the frist 2 words but I know what *test* means. You
got to pass it or you get bad marks. This test looked easy
becaus I coud see the picturs. Only this time she dint want me
to tell her the picturs. That mixd me up. I said the man
yesterday said I shoud tell him that I saw in the ink she said
that dont make no difrence. She said make up storys about the
pepul in the picturs.

I told her how can you tell storys about pepul you never
met. I said why shud I make up lies. I never tell lies any more
becaus I always get caut.

She told me this test and the other one the raw-shok was for getting personalty. I laffed so hard. I said how can you get that thing from inkblots and fotos. She got sore and put her picturs away. I dont care. It was sily. I gess I faled that test too.

Later some men in white coats took me to a difernt part of the hospitil and gave me a game to play. It was like a race with a white mouse. They called the mouse Algernon. Algernon was in a box with a lot of twists and turns like all kinds of walls and they gave me a pencil and a paper with lines and lots of boxes. On one side it said START and on the other end it said FINISH. They said it was *amazed* and that Algernon and me had the same *amazed* to do. I dint see how we could have the same *amazed* if Algernon had a box and I had a paper but I dint say nothing. Anyway there wasnt time because the race started.

One of the men had a watch he was trying to hide so I wouldnt see it so I tryed not to look and that made me nervus.

Anyway that test made me feel worser than all the others because they did it over 10 times with difernt *amazeds* and Algernon won every time. I dint know that mice were so smart. Maybe thats because Algernon is a white mouse. Maybe white mice are smarter then other mice.

progri riport 4 – Mar 8

Their going to use me! Im so excited I can hardly write. Dr Nemur and Dr Strauss had a argament about it first. Dr Nemur was in the office when Dr Strauss brot me in. Dr Nemur was worryed about using me but Dr Strauss told him Miss Kinnian rekemmended me the best from all the people who she was teaching. I like Miss Kinnian becaus shes a very smart teacher. And she said Charlie your going to have a second chance. If you volenteer for this experiment you mite get smart. They dont know if it will be perminint but theirs a chance. Thats why I said ok even when I was scared because she said it was an operashun. She said dont be scared Charlie you done so much with so little I think you deserv it most of all.

So I got scaird when Dr Nemur and Dr Strauss argud about it. Dr Strauss said I had something that was very good. He said I had a good *motor-vation*. I never even knew I had that. I felt proud when he said that not every body with an eye-q of 68 had that thing. I dont know what it is or where I got it but he

said Algernon had it too. Algernons *motor-vation* is the cheese
they put in his box. But it cant be that because I didnt eat any
cheese this week.

Then he told Dr Nemur something I dint understand so
while they were talking I wrote down some of the words.

He said Dr Nemur I know Charlie is not what you had in
mind as the first of your new brede of intelek** (coudnt get the
word) syperman. But most people of his low ment** are host**
and uncoop** they are usualy dull apath** and hard to reach.
He has a good natcher hes intristed and eager to please.

Dr Nemur said remember he will be the first human beeng
ever to have his intelijence trippled by surgicle meens.

Dr Strauss said exakly. Look at how well hes lerned to read
and write for his low mentel age its as grate an acheve** as you
and I lerning einstines therey of **vity without help. That
shows the intenss motor-vation. Its comparat** a temen**
achev** I say we use Charlie.

I dint get all the words and they were talking to fast but it
sounded like Dr Strauss was on my side and like the other one
wasnt.

Then Dr Nemur nodded he said all right maybe your right.
We will use Charlie. When he said that I got so exited I jumped
up and shook his hand for being so good to me. I told him
thank you doc you wont be sorry for giving me a second
chance. And I mean it like I told him. After the operashun Im
gonna try to be smart. Im gonna try awful hard.

progris ript 5 – Mar 10
Im skared. Lots of people who work here and the nurses and
the people who gave me the tests came to bring me candy and
wish me luck. I hop I have luck. I got my rabits foot and my
lucky penny and my horse shoe. Only a black cat crossed me
when I was comming to the hospital. Dr Strauss says dont be
supersitis Charlie this is sience. Anyway Im keeping my rabits
foot with me.

I asked Dr Strauss if Ill beat Algernon in the race after the
operashun and he said may be. If the operashun works Ill
show that mouse I can be as smart as he is. Maybe smarter.
Then Ill be abel to read better and spell the words good and

know lots of things and be like other people. I want to be smart like other people. If it works perminint they will make everybody smart all over the wurld.

They dint give me anything to eat this morning. I dont know what that eating has to do with getting smart. Im very hungry and Dr Nemur took away my box of candy. That Dr Nemur is a grouch. Dr Strauss says I can have it back after the operashun. You cant eat befor a operashun . . .

Progress Report 6 – Mar 15

The operashun dint hurt. He did it while I was sleeping. They took off the bandijis from my eyes and my head today so I can make a PROGRESS REPORT. Dr Nemur who looked at some of my other ones says I spell PROGRESS wrong and he told me how to spell it and REPORT too. I got to try and remember that.

I have a very bad memary for spelling. Dr Strauss says its ok to tell about all the things that happin to me but he says I shoud tell more about what I feel and what I think. When I told him I dont know how to think he said try. All the time when the bandijis were on my eyes I tryed to think. Nothing happened. I dont know what to think about. Maybe if I ask him he will tell me how I can think now that Im suppose to get smart. What do smart people think about. Fancy things I suppose. I wish I knew some fancy things alredy.

Progress Report 7 – mar 19

Nothing is happining. I had lots of tests and different kinds of races with Algernon. I hate that mouse. He always beats me. Dr Strauss said I got to play those games. And he said some time I got to take those tests over again. Thse inkblots are stupid. And those pictures are stupid too. I like to draw a picture of a man and a woman but I wont make up lies about people.

I got a headache from trying to think so much. I thot Dr Strauss was my frend but he dont help me. He dont tell me what to think or when Ill get smart. Miss Kinnian dint come to see me. I think writing these progress reports are stupid too.

Progress Report 8 – Mar 23

Im going back to work at the factery. They said it was better I

shud go back to work but I cant tell anyone what the
operashun was for and I have to come to the hospitil for an
hour evry night after work. They are gonna pay me mony
every month for lerning to be smart.

Im glad Im going back to work because I miss my job and
all my frends and all the fun we have there.

Dr Strauss says I shud keep writing things down but I dont
have to do it every day just when I think of something or
something speshul happins. He says dont get discoridged
because it takes time and it happins slow. He says it took a
long time for Algernon before he got 3 times smarter then he
was before. Thats why Algernon beats me all the time because
he had that operashun too. That makes me feel better. I coud
probly do that *amazed* faster than a reglar mouse. Maybe some
day Ill beat Algernon. Boy that would be something. So far
Algernon looks like he mite be smart perminent.

Mar 25 (I dont have to write PROGRESS REPORT on top any more
just when I hand it in once a week for Dr Nemur to read. I just
have to put the date on. That saves time)

We had a lot of fun at the factery today. Joe Carp said hey
look where Charlie had his operashun what did they do
Charlie put some brains in. I was going to tell him but I
remembered Dr Strauss said no. Then Frank Reilly said what
did you do Charlie forget your key and open your door the
hard way. That made me laff. Their really my frends and they
like me.

Sometimes somebody will say hey look at Joe or Frank or
George he really pulled a Charlie Gordon. I don't know why
they say that but they always laff. This morning Amos Borg
who is the 4 man at Donnegans used my name when he
shouted at Ernie the office boy. Ernie lost a packige. He said
Ernie for godsake what are you trying to be a Charlie Gordon.
I dont understand why he said that. I never lost any packiges.

Mar 28 Dr Strauss came to my room tonight to see why I dint
come in like I was suppose to. I told him I dont like to race
with Algernon any more. He said I dont have to for a while but
I shud come in. He had a present for me only it wasnt a

present but just for lend. I thot it was a little television but it wasnt. He said I got to turn it on when I go to sleep. I said your kidding why shud I turn it on when Im going to sleep. Who ever herd of a thing like that. But he said if I want to get smart I got to do what he says. I told him I dint think I was going to get smart and he put his hand on my sholder and said Charlie you dont know it yet but your getting smarter all the time. You wont notice for a while. I think he was just being nice to make me feel good because I dont look any smarter.

Oh yes I almost forget. I asked him when I can go back to the class at Miss Kinnian school. He said I wont go their. He said that soon Miss Kinnian will come to the hospitil to start and teach me speshul. I was mad at her for not comming to see me when I got the operashun but I like her so may be we will be frends again.

Mar 29 That crazy TV kept me up all night. How can I sleep with something yelling crazy things all night in my ears. And the nutty pictures. Wow. I dont know what it says when Im up so how am I going to know when Im sleeping.

Dr Strauss says its ok. He says my brains are lerning when I sleep and that will help me when Miss Kinnian starts my lessons in the hospitl (only I found out it isnt a hospitil its a laboratory). I think its all crazy. If you can get smart when your sleeping why do people go to school. That thing I dont think will work. I use to watch the late show and the late late show on TV all the time and it never made me smart. Maybe you have to sleep while you watch it.

PROGRESS REPORT 9 – April 3

Dr Strauss showed me how to keep the TV turned low so now I can sleep. I dont hear a thing. And I still dont understand what it says. A few times I play it over in the morning to find out what I lerned when I was sleeping and I dont think so. Miss Kinnian says Maybe its another langwidge or something. But most times it sounds american. It talks so fast faster than even Miss Gold who was my teacher in 6 grade and I remember she talked so fast I coudnt understand her.

I told Dr Strauss what good is it to get smart in my sleep. I want to be smart when Im awake. He says its the same thing and I have two minds. Theres the *subconscious* and the *conscious* (thats how you spell it). And one dont tell the other one what its doing. They dont even talk to each other. Thats why I dream. And boy have I been having crazy dreams. Wow. Ever since that night TV. The late late late late late show.

I forgot to ask him if it was only me or if everybody had those two minds.

(I just looked up the word in the dictionary Dr Strauss gave me. The word is *subconscious. adj. Of the nature of mental operations yet not present in consciousness; as, subconscious conflict of desires.*) Theres more but I still dont know what it means. This isnt a very good dictionary for dumb people like me.

Anyway the headache is from the party. My frends from the factery Joe Carp and Frank Reilly invited me to go with them to Muggsys Saloon for some drinks. I dont like to drink but they said we will have lots of fun. I had a good time.

Joe Carp said I shoud show the girls how I mop out the toilet in the factory and he got me a mop. I showed them and everyone laffed when I told that Mr Donnegan said I was the best janiter he ever had because I like my job and do it good and never come late or miss a day except for my operashun.

I said Miss Kinnian always said Charlie be proud of your job because you do it good.

Everybody laffed and we had a good time and they gave me lots of drinks and Joe said Charlie is a card when hes potted. I dont know what that means but everybody likes me and we have fun. I cant wait to be smart like my best frends Joe Carp and Frank Reilly.

I dont remember how the party was over but I think I went out to buy a newspaper and coffe for Joe and Frank and when I came back there was no one their. I looked for them all over till late. Then I dont remember so good but I think I got sleepy or sick. A nice cop brot me back home. Thats what my landlady Mrs Flynn says.

But I got a headache and a big lump on my head and black and blue all over. I think maybe I fell but Joe Carp says it was the cop they beat up drunks some times. I dont think so. Miss Kinnian says cops are to help people. Anyway I got a bad headache and Im sick and hurt all over. I dont think Ill drink anymore.

April 6 I beat Algernon! I dint even know I beat him until Burt the tester told me. Then the second time I lost because I got so exited I fell off the chair before I finished. But after that I beat him 8 more times. I must be getting smart to beat a smart mouse like Algernon. But I dont *feel* smarter.

I wanted to race Algernon some more but Burt said thats enough for one day. They let me hold him for a minit. Hes not so bad. Hes soft like a ball of cotton. He blinks and when he opens his eyes their black and pink on the eges.

I said can I feed him because I felt bad to beat him and I wanted to be nice and make frends. Burt said no Algernon is a very specshul mouse with an operashun like mine, and he was the first of all the animals to stay smart so long. He told me Algernon is so smart that every day he has to solve a test to get his food. Its a thing like a lock on a door that changes every time Algernon goes in to eat so he has to lern something new to get his food. That made me sad because if he couldnt lern he would be hungry.

I dont think its right to make you pass a test to eat. How would Dr Nemur like it to have to pass a test every time he wants to eat. I think Ill be frends with Algernon.

April 9 Tonight after work Miss Kinnian was at the laboratory. She looked like she was glad to see me but scared. I told her dont worry Miss Kinnian Im not smart yet and she laffed. She said I have confidence in you Charlie the way you struggled so hard to read and right better than all the others. At werst you will have it for a littel wile and your doing somthing for sience.

We are reading a very hard book. I never read such a hard book before. Its called *Robinson Crusoe* about a man who gets merooned on a dessert Iland. Hes smart and figers out all kinds of things so he can have a house and food and hes a good swimmer. Only I feel sorry because hes all alone and has no frends. But I think their must be somebody else on the iland because theres a picture with his funny umbrella looking at footprints. I hope he gets a frend and not be lonely.

April 10 Miss Kinnian teaches me to spell better. She says look at a word and close your eyes and say it over and over until you remember. I have lots of truble with *through* that you say *threw* and *enough* and *tough* that you dont say *enew* and *tew*. You got to say *enuff* and *tuff*. Thats how I use to write it before I started to get smart. Im confused but Miss Kinnian says theres no reason in spelling.

Apr 14 Finished *Robinson Crusoe*. I want to find out more about what happens to him but Miss Kinnian says that's all there is. *Why*.

Apr 15 Miss Kinnian says Im lerning fast. She read some of the Progress Reports and she looked at me kind of funny. She says Im a fine person and Ill show them all. I asked her why. She said never mind but I shoudnt feel bad if I find out that everybody inst nice like I think. She said for a person who god gave so little to you done more then a lot of people with brains they never even used. I said all my frends are smart people but there good. They like me and they never did anything that wasnt nice. Then she got something in her eye and she had to run out to the ladys room.

Apr 16 Today, I lerned, the *comma,* this is a comma (,) a period, with a tail, Miss Kinnian, says its importent, because, it makes writing better, she said, somebody, coud lose, a lot of money, if a comma, isnt, in the, right place, I dont have, any money, and I dont see, how a comma, keeps you from losing it,
   But she says, everybody, uses commas, so Ill use, them too,

Apr 17 I used the comma wrong. Its punctuation. Miss Kinnian told me to look up long words in the dictionary to lern to spell them. I said whats the difference if yu can read it anyway. She said its part of your education so now on Ill look up all the words Im not sure how to spell. It takes a long time to write that way but I think Im remembering. I only have to look up once and after that I get it right. Anyway thats how come I got the word *punctuation* right. (Its that way in the dictionary). Miss Kinnian says a period is punctuation too, and there are

lots of other marks to lern. I told her I thot all the periods had
to have tails but she said no.

You got to mix them up, she showed? me" how. to mix!
them (up,. and now; I can! mix up all kinds" of punctuation,
in ! my writing? There, are lots! of rules? to lern; but Im gettin'g
them in my head.

One thing I? like about, Dear Miss Kinnian: (thats the way it
goes in a business letter if I ever go into business) is she,
always gives me" a reason' when – I ask. She's a gen'ius! I
wish! I cou'd be smart' like, her; (Punctuation, is; fun!)

April 18 What a dope I am! I didn't even understand what she
was talking about. I read the grammar book last night and it
explanes the whole thing. Then I saw it was the same way as
Miss Kinnian was trying to tell me, but I didn't get it. I got up
in the middle of the night, and the whole thing straightened
out in my mind.

Miss Kinnian said that the TV working in my sleep helped out.
She said I reached a plateau. Thats like the flat top of a hill.

After I figgered out how punctuation worked, I read over all
my old Progress Reports from the beginning. Boy, did I have
crazy spelling and punctuation! I told Miss Kinnian I ought to
go over the pages and fix all the mistakes but she said , 'No,
Charlie, Dr Nemur wants them just as they are. That's why he
let you keep them after they were photostated, to see your
own progress. You're coming along fast, Charlie.'

That me feel good. After the lesson I went down and played
with Algernon. We don't race any more.

April 20 I feel sick inside. Not sick like for a doctor, but inside
my chest it feels empty like getting punched and a heartburn at
the same time.

I wasn't going to write about it, but I guess I got to, because
it's important. Today was the first time I ever stayed home from
work.

Last night Joe Carp and Frank Reilly invited me to a party.
There were lots of girls and some men from the factory. I
remembered how sick I got last time I drank too much, so I
told Joe I didn't want anything to drink. He gave me a plain

Coke instead. It tasted funny, but I thought it was just a bad taste in my mouth.

We had a lot of fun for a while. Joe said I should dance with Ellen and she would teach me the steps. I fell a few times and I couldn't understand why because no one else was dancing besides Ellen and me. And all the time I was tripping because somebody's foot was always sticking out.

Then when I got up I saw the look on Joe's face and it gave me a funny feeling in my stomack. 'He's a scream,' one of the girls said. Everybody was laughing.

Frank said, 'I ain't laughed so much since we sent him off for the newspaper that night at Muggsy's and ditched him.'

'Look at him. His face is red.'

'He's blushing. Charlie is blushing.'

'Hey, Ellen, what'd you do to Charlie? I never saw him act like that before.'

I didn't know what to do or where to turn. Everyone was looking at me and laughing and I felt naked. I wanted to hide myself. I ran out into the street and I threw up. Then I walked home. It's a funny thing I never knew that Joe and Frank and the others liked to have me around all the time to make fun of me.

Now I know what it means when they say 'to pull a Charlie Gordon.' I'm ashamed.

PROGRESS REPORT 11

April 21 Still didn't go into the factory. I told Mrs. Flynn my landlady to call and tell Mr. Donnegan I was sick. Mrs. Flynn looks at me very funny lately like she's scared of me.

I think it's a good thing about finding out how everybody laughs at me. I thought about it a lot. It's because I'm so dumb and I don't even know when I'm doing something dumb. People think it's funny when a dumb person can't do things the same way they can.

Anyway, now I know I'm getting smarter every day. I know punctuation and I can spell good. I like to look up the hard words in the dictionary and I remember them. I'm reading a lot now, and Miss Kinnian says I read very fast. Sometimes I even understand what I'm reading about, and it stays in my mind.

There are times when I can close my eyes and think of a page and it all comes back like a picture.

Besides history, geography, and arithmetic, Miss Kinnian said I should start to learn a few foreign languages. Dr. Strauss gave me some more tapes to play while I sleep. I still don't understand how that conscious and unconscious mind works, but Dr. Strauss says not to worry yet. He asked me to promise that when I start learning college subjects next week I wouldn't read any books on psychology – that is, until he gives me permission.

I feel a lot better today, but I guess I'm still a little angry that all the time people were laughing and making fun of me because I wasn't so smart. When I become intelligent like Dr. Strauss says, with three times my I.Q. of 68, then maybe I'll be like everyone else and people will like me and be friendly.

I'm not sure what an I.Q. is. Dr. Nemur said it was something that measured how intelligent you were – like a scale in the drug-store weighs pounds. But Dr. Strauss had a big argument with him and said an I.Q. didn't weigh intelligence at all. He said an I.Q. showed how much intelligence you could get, like the numbers on the outside of a measuring cup. You still had to fill the cup up with stuff.

Then when I asked Burt, who gives me my intelligence tests and works with Algernon, he said that both of them were wrong (only I had to promise not to tell them he said so). Burt says that the I.Q. measures a lot of different things including some of the things you learned already, and it really isn't any good at all.

So I still don't know what I.Q. is except that mine is going to be over 200 soon. I didn't want to say anything, but I don't see how if they don't know *what* it is, or *where* it is – I don't see how they know *how much* of it you've got.

Dr. Nemur says I have to take a *Rorschach Test* tomorrow. I wonder what *that* is.

April 22 I found out what a *Rorschach* is. It's the test I took before the operation – the one with the inkblots on the pieces of cardboard. The man who gave me the test was the same one.

I was scared to death of those inkblots. I knew he was going to ask me to find the pictures and I knew I wouldn't be able to. I was thinking to myself, if only there was some way of knowing what kind of pictures were hidden there. Maybe there weren't any pictures at all. Maybe it was just a trick to see if I was dumb enough to look for something that wasn't there. Just thinking about that made me sore at him.

'All right, Charlie,' he said, 'you've seen these cards before, remember?'

'Of course I remember.'

The way I said it, he knew I was angry, and he looked surprised. 'Yes, of course. Now I want you to look at this one. What might this be? What do you see on this card? People see all sorts of things in these inkblots. Tell me what it might be for you – what it makes you think of.'

I was shocked. That wasn't what I had expected him to say at all. 'You mean there are no pictures hidden in those inkblots?'

He frowned and took off his glasses. 'What?'

'Pictures. Hidden in the inkblots. Last time you told me that everyone could see them and you wanted me to find them too.'

He explained to me that the last time he had used almost the exact same words he was using now. I didn't believe it, and I still have the suspicion that he misled me at the time just for the fun of it. Unless – I don't know any more – could I have been *that* feebleminded?

We went through the cards slowly. One of them looked like a pair of bats tugging at something. Another one looked like two men fencing with swords. I imagined all sorts of things. I guess I got carried away. But I didn't trust him any more, and I kept turning them around and even looking on the back to see if there was anything there I was supposed to catch. While he ws making his notes, I peeked out of the corner of my eye to read it. But it was all in code that looked like this:

WF + A Ddf – Ad orig. WF – A SF + obj

The test still doesn't make sense to me. It seems to me that anyone could make up lies about things that they didn't really see. How could he know I wasn't making a fool of him by mentioning things that I didn't really imagine? Maybe I'll understand it when Dr. Strauss lets me read up on psychology.

April 25 I figured out a new way to line up the machines in the factory, and Mr. Donnegan says it will save him ten thousand dollars a year in labor and increased production. He gave me a twenty-five-dollar bonus.

I wanted to take Joe Carp and Frank Reilly out to lunch to celebrate, but Joe said he had to buy some things for his wife, and Frank said he was meeting his cousin for lunch. I guess it'll take a little time for them to get used to the changes in me. Everybody seems to be frightened of me. When I went over to Amos Borg and tapped him on the shoulder, he jumped up in the air.

People don't talk to me much any more or kid around the way they used to. It makes the job kind of lonely.

April 27 I got up the nerve today to ask Miss Kinnian to have dinner with me tomorrow night to celebrate my bonus.

At first she wasn't sure it was right, but I asked Dr. Strauss and he said it was okay. Dr. Strauss and Dr. Nemur don't seem to be getting along so well. They're arguing all the time. This evening when I came in to ask Dr. Strauss about having dinner with Miss Kinnian, I heard them shouting. Dr. Nemur was saying that it was *his* experiment and *his* research, and Dr. Strauss was shouting back that he contributed just as much, because he found me through Miss Kinnian and he performed the operation. Dr. Strauss said that someday thousands of neurosurgeons might be using his technique all over the world.

Dr. Nemur wanted to publish the results of the experiment at the end of this month. Dr. Strauss wanted to wait a while longer to be sure. Dr. Strauss said that Dr. Nemur was more interested in the Chair of Psychology at Princeton than he was in the experiment. Dr. Nemur said that Dr. Strauss was nothing but an opportunist who was trying to ride to glory on *his* coattails.

When I left afterwards, I found myself trembling. I don't know why for sure, but it was as if I'd seen both men clearly for the first time. I remember hearing Burt say that Dr. Nemur had a shrew of a wife who was pushing him all the time to get

things published so that he could become famous. Burt said
that the dream of her life was to have a big-shot husband.

Was Dr. Strauss really trying to ride on his coattails?

April 28 I don't understand why I never noticed how beautiful
Miss Kinnian really is. She has brown eyes and feathery brown
hair that comes to the top of her neck. She's only thirty-four! I
think from the beginning I had the feeling that she was an
unreachable genius – and very, very old. Now, every time I see
her she grows younger and more lovely.

We had dinner and a long talk. When she said that I was
coming along so fast that soon I'd be leaving her behind, I
laughed.

'It's true, Charlie. You're already a better reader than I am.
You can read a whole page at a glance while I can take in only
a few lines at a time. And you remember every single thing
you read. I'm lucky if I can recall the main thoughts and the
general meaning.'

'I don't feel intelligent. There are so many things I don't
understand.'

She took out a cigarette and I lit it for her. 'You've got to be
a *little* patient. You're accomplishing in days and weeks what it
takes normal people to do in half a lifetime. That's what makes
it so amazing. You're like a giant sponge now, soaking things
in. Facts, figures, general knowledge. And soon you'll begin to
connect them, too. You'll see how the different branches of
learning are related. There are many levels, Charlie, like steps
on a giant ladder that take you up higher and higher to see
more and more of the world around you.

'I can see only a little bit of that, Charlie, and I won't go
much higher than I am now, but you'll keep climbing up and
up, and see more and more, and each step will open new
worlds that you never even knew existed.' She frowned. 'I
hope . . . I just hope to God –'

'What?'

'Never mind, Charles. I just hope I wasn't wrong to advise
you to go into this in the first place.'

I laughed. 'How could that be? It worked, didn't it? Even
Algernon is still smart.'

We sat there silently for a while and I knew what she was thinking about as she watched me toying with the chain of my rabbit's foot and my keys. I didn't want to think of that possibility any more than elderly people want to think of death. I *knew* that this was only the beginning. I knew what she meant about levels because I'd seen some of them already. The thought of leaving her behind made me sad.

I'm in love with Miss Kinnian.

PROGRESS REPORT 12

April 30 I've quit my job with Donnegan's Plastic Box Company. Mr. Donnegan insisted that it would be better for all concerned if I left. What did I do to make them hate me so?

The first I knew of it was when Mr. Donnegan showed me the petition. Eight hundred and forty names, everyone connected with the factory, except Fanny Girden. Scanning the list quickly, I saw at once that hers was the only missing name. All the rest demanded that I be fired.

Joe Carp and Frank Reilly wouldn't talk to me about it. No one else would either, except Fanny. She was one of the few people I'd known who set her mind to something and believed it no matter what the rest of the world proved, said, or did – and Fanny did not believe that I should have been fired. She had been against the petition on principle and despite the pressure and threats she'd held out.

'Which don't mean to say,' she remarked, 'that I don't think there's something mighty strange about you, Charlie. Them changes. I don't know. You used to be a good, dependable, ordinary man – not too bright maybe, but honest. Who knows what you done to yourself to get so smart all of a sudden. Like everybody around here's been saying, Charlie, it's not right.'

'But how can you say that, Fanny? What's wrong with a man becoming intelligent and wanting to acquire knowledge and understanding of the world around him?'

She stared down at her work and I turned to leave. Without looking at me, she said: 'It was evil when Eve listened to the snake and ate from the tree of knowledge. It was evil when she saw that she was naked. If not for that none of us would ever have to grow old and sick, and die.'

Once again now I have the feeling of shame burning inside me. This intelligence has driven a wedge between me and all the people I once knew and loved. Before, they laughed at me and despised me for my ignorance and dullness; now, they hate me for my knowledge and understanding. What in God's name do they want of me?

They've driven me out of the factory. Now I'm more alone than ever before . . .

May 15 Dr. Strauss is very angry at me for not having written any progress reports in two weeks. He's justified because the lab is now paying me a regular salary. I told him I was too busy thinking and reading. When I pointed out that writing was such a slow process that it made me impatient with my poor handwriting, he suggested that I learn to type. It's much easier to write now because I can type nearly seventy-five words a minute. Dr. Strauss continually reminds me of the need to speak and write simply so that people will be able to understand me.

I'll try to review all the things that happened to me during the last two weeks. Algernon and I were presented to the American Psychological Association sitting in convention with the World Psychological Association last Tuesday. We created quite a sensation. Dr. Nemur and Dr. Strauss were proud of us.

I suspect that Dr. Nemur, who is sixty – ten years older than Dr. Strauss – finds it necessary to see tangible results of his work. Undoubtedly the result of pressure by Mrs. Nemur.

Contrary to my earlier impressions of him, I realize that Dr. Nemur is not at all a genius. He has a very good mind, but it struggles under the specter of self-doubt. He wants people to take him for a genius. Therefore, it is important for him to feel that his work is accepted by the world. I believe that Dr. Nemur was afraid of further delay because he worried that someone else might make a discovery along these lines and take the credit from him.

Dr. Strauss on the other hand might be called a genius, although I feel that his areas of knowledge are too limited. He was educated in the tradition of narrow specialization; the broader aspects of background were neglected far more than necessary – even for a neuro-surgeon.

I was shocked to learn that the only ancient languages he could read were Latin, Greek, and Hebrew, and that he knows almost nothing of mathematics beyond the elementary levels of the calculus of variations. When he admitted this to me, I found myself almost annoyed. It was as if he'd hidden this part of himself in order to deceive me, pretending – as do many people I've discovered – to be what he is not. No one I've ever known is what he appears to be on the surface.

Dr. Nemur appears to be uncomfortable around me. Sometimes when I try to talk to him, he just looks at me strangely and turns away. I was angry at first when Dr. Strauss told me I was giving Dr. Nemur an inferiority complex. I thought he was mocking me and I'm oversensitive at being made fun of.

How was I to know that a highly respected psycho-experimentalist like Nemur was unacquainted with Hindustani and Chinese? It's absurd when you consider the work that is being done in India and China today in the very field of his study.

I asked Dr. Strauss how Nemur could refute Rahajamati's attack on his method and results if Nemur couldn't even read them in the first place. That strange look on Dr. Strauss' face can mean only one of two things. Either he doesn't want to tell Nemur what they're saying in India, or else – and this worries me – Dr. Strauss doesn't know either. I must be careful to speak and write clearly and simply so that people won't laugh.

May 18 I am very disturbed. I saw Miss Kinnian last night for the first time in over a week. I tried to avoid all discussions of intellectual concepts and to keep the conversation on a simple, everyday level, but she just stared at me blankly and asked me what I meant about the mathematical variance equivalent in Dorbermann's *Fifth Concerto*.

When I tried to explain she stopped me and laughed. I guess I got angry, but I suspect I'm approaching her on the wrong level. No matter what I try to discuss with her, I am unable to communicate. I must review Vrostadt's equations on *Levels of Semantic Progression*. I find that I don't communicate with people much any more. Thank God for books and music and things I can think about. I am alone in my apartment at Mrs. Flynn's boardinghouse most of the time and seldom speak to anyone.

May 20 I would not have noticed the new dishwasher, a boy of about sixteen, at the corner diner where I take my evening meals if not for the incident of the broken dishes.

They crashed to the floor, shattering and sending bits of white china under the tables. The boy stood there, dazed and frightened, holding the empty tray in his hand. The whistles and catcalls from the customers (the cries of 'hey, there go the profits!' . . . *'Mazeltov!'* . . . and 'well, *he* didn't work here very long . . .' which invariably seem to follow the breaking of glass or dishware in a public restaurant) all seemed to confuse him.

When the owner came to see what the excitement was about, the boy cowered as if he expected to be struck and threw up his arms as if to ward off the blow.

'All right! All right, you dope,' shouted the owner, 'don't just stand there! Get the broom and sweep that mess up. A broom . . . a broom, you idiot! It's in the kitchen. Sweep up all the pieces.'

The boy saw that he was not going to be punished. His frightened expression disappeared and he smiled and hummed as he came back with the broom to sweep the floor. A few of the rowdier customers kept up the remarks, amusing themselves at his expense.

'Here, sonny, over here there's a nice piece behind you . . '

'C'mon, do it again . . . '

'He's not so dumb. It's easier to break 'em than to wash 'em . . . '

As his vacant eyes moved across the crowd of amused onlookers, he slowly mirrored their smiles and finally broke into an uncertain grin at the joke which he obviously did not understand.

I felt sick inside as I looked at his dull, vacuous smile, the wide, bright eyes of a child, uncertain but eager to please. They were laughing at him because he was mentally retarded.

And I had been laughing at him too.

Suddenly, I was furious at myself and all those who were smirking at him. I jumped up and shouted, 'Shut up! Leave him alone! It's not his fault he can't understand! He can't help what he is! But for God's sake . . . he's still a human being!'

The room grew silent. I cursed myself for losing control and creating a scene. I tried not to look at the boy as I paid my check and walked out without touching my food. I felt ashamed for both of us.

How strange it is that people of honest feelings and sensibility, who would not take advantage of a man born without arms or legs or eyes – how such people think nothing of abusing a man born with low intelligence. It infuriated me to think that not too long ago I, like this boy, had foolishly played the clown.

And I had almost forgotten.

I'd hidden the picture of the old Charlie Gordon from myself because now that I was intelligent it was something that had to be pushed out of my mind. But today in looking at that boy, for the first time I saw what I had been. *I was just like him!*

Only a short time ago, I learned that people laughed at me. Now I can see that unknowingly I joined with them in laughing at myself. That hurts most of all.

I have often reread my progress reports and seen the illiteracy, the childish naïveté, the mind of low intelligence peering from a dark room, through the keyhole, at the dazzling light outside. I see that even in my dullness I knew that I was inferior, and that other people had something I lacked – something denied me. In my mental blindness, I thought that it was somehow connected with the ability to read and write, and I was sure that if I could get those skills I would automatically have intelligence too.

Even a feeble-minded man wants to be like other men.

A child may not know how to feed itself, or what to eat, yet it knows of hunger.

This then is what I was like. I never knew. Even with my gift of intellectual awareness, I never really knew.

This day was good for me. Seeing the past more clearly, I have decided to use my knowledge and skills to work in the field of increasing human intelligence levels. Who is better equipped for this work? Who else has lived in both worlds? These are my people. Let me use my gift to do something for them.

Tomorrow, I will discuss with Dr. Strauss the manner in which I can work in this area. I may be able to help him work out the problems of widespread use of the technique which was used on me. I have several good ideas of my own.

There is so much that might be done with this technique. If I could be made into a genius, what about thousands of others like myself? What fantastic levels might be achieved by using this technique on normal people? On *geniuses?*

There are so many doors to open. I am impatient to begin.

PROGRESS REPORT 13

May 23 It happened today. Algernon bit me. I visited the lab to see him as I do occasionally, and when I took him out of his cage, he snapped at my hand. I put him back and watched him for a while. He was unusually disturbed and vicious.

May 24 Burt, who is in charge of the experimental animals, tells me that Algernon is changing. He is less co-operative, he refuses to run the maze any more; general motivation has decreased. And he hasn't been eating. Everyone is upset about what this may mean.

May 25 They've been feeding Algernon, who now refuses to work the shifting-lock problem. Everyone identifies me with Algernon. In a way we're both the first of our kind. They're all pretending that Algernon's behaviour is not necessarily significant for me. But it's hard to hide the fact that some of the other animals who were used in this experiment are showing strange behavior.

Dr. Strauss and Dr. Nemur have asked me not to come to the lab any more. I know what they're thinking but I can't accept it. I am going ahead with my plans to carry their research forward. With all due respect to both of these fine scientists, I am well aware of their limitations. If there is an answer, I'll have to find it out for myself. Suddenly, time has become very important to me.

May 29 I have been given a lab of my own and permission to go ahead with the research. I'm on to something. Working day and night. I've had a cot moved into the lab. Most of my writing time is spent on the notes which I keep in a separate folder, but from time to time I feel it necessary to put down my moods and my thoughts out of sheer habit.

I find the *calculus of intelligence* to be a fascinating study. Here is the place for the application of all the knowledge I have acquired. In a sense it's the problem I've been concerned with all my life.

May 31 Dr. Strauss thinks I'm working too hard. Dr. Nemur says I'm trying to cram a lifetime of research and thought into a few weeks. I know I should rest, but I'm driven on by something inside that won't let me stop. I've got to find the reason for the sharp regression in Algernon. I've got to know *if* and *when* it will happen to me.

June 4 LETTER TO DR. STRAUSS *(copy)*
Dear Dr. Strauss:

Under separate cover I am sending you a copy of my report entitled, 'The Algernon-Gordon Effect: A Study of Structure and Function of Increased Intelligence,' which I would like to have you read and have published.

As you see, my experiments are completed. I have included in my report all of my formulae, as well as mathematical analysis in the appendix. Of course, these should be verified.

Because of its importance of both you and Dr. Nemur (and need I say to myself, too?) I have checked and re-checked my results a dozen times in the hope of finding an error. I am sorry to say the results must stand. Yet for the sake of science, I am grateful for the little bit that I here add to the knowledge of the function of the human mind and of the laws governing the artificial increase of human intelligence.

I recall your once saying to me that an experimental *failure* or the *disproving* of a theory was as important to the advancement of learning as a success would be. I know now that this is true. I am sorry, however, that my own contribution

to the field must rest upon the ashes of the work of two men I
regard so highly.

Yours truly,
Charles Gordon

encl.: rept.

June 5 I must not become emotional. The facts and results of
my experiments are clear, and the more sensational aspects of
my own rapid climb cannot obscure the fact that the tripling of
intelligence by the surgical technique developed by Drs.
Strauss and Nemur must be viewed as having little or no
practical applicability (at the present time) to the increase of
human intelligence.

As I review the records and data on Algernon, I see that
although he is still in his physical infancy, he has regressed
mentally. Motor activity is impaired; there is a general
reduction of glandular activity; there is an accelerated loss of
co-ordination.

There are also strong indications of progressive amnesia.

As will be seen by my report, these and other physical and
mental deterioration syndromes can be predicted with
statistically significant results by the application of my formula.

The surgical stimulus to which we were both subjected has
resulted in an intensification and acceleration of all mental
processes. The unforeseen development, which I have taken
the liberty of calling the *Algernon–Gordon Effect*, is the logical
extension of the entire intelligence speed-up. The hypothesis
here proven may be described simply in the following terms:
Artificially increased intelligence deteriorates at a rate of time
directly proportional to the quantity of the increase.

I feel that this, in itself, is an important discovery.

As long as I am able to write, I will continue to record my
thoughts in these progress reports. It is one of my few
pleasures. However, by all indications, my own mental
deterioration will be very rapid.

I have already begun to notice signs of emotional instability
and forgetfulness, the first symptoms of the burnout.

June 10 Deterioration progressing. I have become absent-minded. Algernon died two days ago. Dissection shows my predictions were right. His brain had decreased in weight and there was a general smoothing out of cerebral convolutions as well as a deepening and broadening of brain fissures.

I guess the same thing is or will soon be happening to me. Now that it's definite, I don't want it to happen.

I put Algernon's body in a cheese box and buried him in the back yard. I cried.

June 15 Dr. Strauss came to see me again. I wouldn't open the door and I told him to go away. I want to be left to myself. I have become touchy and irritable. I feel the darkness closing in. It's hard to throw off thoughts of suicide. I keep telling myself how important this introspective journal will be.

It's a strange sensation to pick up a book that you've read and enjoyed just a few months ago and discover that you don't remember it. I remembered how great I thought John Milton was, but when I picked up *Paradise Lost* I couldn't understand it at all. I got so angry I threw the book across the room.

I've got to try to hold on to some of it. Some of the things I've learned. Oh, God, please don't take it all away.

June 19 Sometimes, at night, I go out for a walk. Last night I couldn't remember where I lived. A policeman took me home. I have the strange feeling that this has all happened to me before – a long time ago. I keep telling myself I'm the only person in the world who can describe what's happening to me.

June 21 Why can't I remember? I've got to fight. I lie in bed for days and I don't know who or where I am. Then it all comes back to me in a flash. Fugues of amnesia. Symptoms of senility – second childhood. I can watch them coming on. It's so cruelly logical. I learned so much and so fast. Now my mind is deteriorating rapidly. I won't let it happen. I'll fight it. I can't help thinking of the boy in the restaurant, the blank expression, the silly smile, the people laughing at him. No – please – not that again . . .

June 22   I'm forgetting things that I learned recently. It seems to be following the classic pattern – the last things learned are the first things forgotten. Or is that the pattern? I'd better look it up again . . .

I reread my paper on the *Algernon –Gordon Effect* and I get the strange feeling that it was written by someone else. There are parts I don't even understand.

Motor activity impaired. I keep tripping over things, and it becomes increasingly difficult to type.

June 23   I've given up using the typewriter completely. My co-ordination is bad. I feel that I'm moving slower and slower. Had a terrible shock today. I picked up a copy of an article I used in my research, Krueger's *Uber psychische Ganzheit,* to see if it would help me understand what I had done. First I thought there was something wrong with my eyes. Then I realized I could no longer read German. I tested myself in other languages. All gone.

June 30   A week since I dare to write again. It's slipping away like sand through my fingers. Most of the books I have are too hard for me now. I get angry with them because I know that I read and understood them just a few weeks ago.

I keep telling myself I must keep writing these reports so that somebody will know what is happening to me. But it gets harder to form the words and remember spellings. I have to look up even simple words in the dictionary now and it makes me impatient with myself.

Dr. Strauss comes around almost every day, but I told him I wouldn't see or speak to anybody. He feels guilty. They all do. But I don't blame anyone. I knew what might happen. But how it hurts.

July 7   I don't know where the week went. Todays Sunday I know because I can see through my window people going to church. I think I stayed in bed all week but I remember Mrs. Flynn bringing food to me a few times. I keep saying over and over Ive got to do something but then I forget or maybe its just easier not to do what I say Im going to do.

I think of my mother and father a lot these days. I found a picture of them with me taken at a beach. My father has a big ball under his arm and my mother is holding me by the hand. I dont remember them the way they are in the picture. All I remember is my father drunk most of the time and arguing with mom about money.

He never shaved much and he used to scratch my face when he hugged me. My mother said he died but Cousin Miltie said he heard his mom and dad say that my father ran away with another woman. When I asked my mother she slapped my face and said my father was dead. I dont think I ever found out which was true but I dont care much. (He said he was going to take me to see cows on a farm once but he never did. He never kept his promises . . .)

July 10 My landlady Mrs Flynn is very worried about me. She says the way I lay around all day and dont do anything I remind her of her son before she threw him out of the house. She said she doesn't like loafers. If Im sick its one thing, but if Im a loafer thats another thing and she wont have it. I told her I think Im sick.

I try to read a little bit every day, mostly stories, but sometimes I have to read the same thing over and over again because I dont know what it means. And its hard to write. I know I should look up all the words in the dictionary but its so hard and Im so tired all the time.

Then I got the idea that I would only use the easy words instead of the long hard ones. That saves time. I put flowers on Algernons grave about once a week. Mrs Flynn thinks Im crazy to put flowers on a mouses grave but I told her that Algernon was special.

July 14 Its sunday again. I dont have anything to do to keep me busy now because my television set is broke and I dont have any money to get it fixed. (I think I lost this months check from the lab. I dont remember)

I get awful headaches and asperin doesnt help me much. Mrs Flynn knows Im really sick and she feels very sorry for me. Shes a wonderful woman whenever someone is sick.

July 22 Mrs Flynn called a strange doctor to see me. She was afraid I was going to die. I told the doctor I wasnt too sick and that I only forget sometimes. He asked me did I have any friends or relatives and I said no I dont have any. I told him I had a friend called Algernon once but he was a mouse and we used to run races together. He looked at me kind of funny like he thought I was crazy.

He smiled when I told him I used to be a genius. He talked to me like I was a baby and he winked at Mrs Flynn. I got mad and chased him out because he was making fun of me the way they all used to.

July 24 I have no more money and Mrs Flynn says I got to go to work somewhere and pay the rent because I havent paid for over two months. I dont know any work but the job I used to have at Donnegans Plastic Box Company. I dont want to go back there because they all knew me when I was smart and maybe theyll laugh at me. But I don't know what else to do to get money.

July 25 I was looking at some of my old progress reports and its very funny but I cant read what I wrote. I can make out some of the words but they dont make sense.

Miss Kinnian came to the door but I said to go away I dont want to see you. She cried and I cried too but I wouldnt let her in because I didn't want her to laugh at me. I told her I didn't like her any more. I told her I didnt want to be smart any more. Thats not true. I still love her and I still want to be smart but I had to say that so shed go away. She gave Mrs Flynn money to pay the rent. I dont want that. I got to get a job.

Please . . . please let me not forget how to read and write . . . .

July 27 Mr Donnegan was very nice when I came back and asked him for my old job of janitor. First he was very suspicious but I told him what happened to me then he looked very sad and put his hand on my shoulder and said Charlie Gordon you got guts.

Everybody looked at me when I came downstairs and started

working in the toilet sweeping it out like I used to. I told myself Charlie if they make fun of you dont get sore because you remember their not so smart as you once thot they were. And besides they were once your friends and if they laughed at you that doesnt mean anything because they liked you too.

One of the new men who came to work there after I went away made a nasty crack he said hey Charlie I hear your a very smart fella a real quiz kid. Say something intelligent. I felt bad but Joe Carp came over and grabbed him by the shirt and said leave him alone you lousy cracker or Ill break your neck. I didn't expect Joe to take my part so I guess hes really my friend.

Later Frank Reilly came over and said Charlie if anybody bothers you or trys to take advantage you call me or Joe and we will set em straight. I said thanks Frank and I got choked up so I had to turn around and go into the supply room so he wouldn't see me cry. Its good to have friends.

July 28 I did a dumb thing today I forgot I wasnt in Miss Kinnians class at the adult center any more like I use to be. I went in and sat down in my old seat in the back of the room and she looked at me funny and she said Charles. I dint remember she ever called me that before only Charlie so I said hello Miss Kinnian Im redy for my lesin today only I lost my reader that we was using. She startid to cry and run out of the room and everybody looked at me and I saw they wasnt the same pepul who used to be in my class.

Then all of a suddin I remembered some things about the operashun and me getting smart and I said holy smoke I reely pulled a Charlie Gordon that time. I went away before she come back to the room.

Thats why Im going away from New York for good. I dont want to do nothing like that agen. I dont want Miss Kinnian to feel sorry for me. Evry body feels sorry at the factery and I dont want that eather so Im going someplace where nobody knows that Charlie Gordon was once a genus and now he cant even reed a book or rite good.

Im taking a cuple of books along and even if I cant reed them Ill practise hard and maybe I wont forget every thing I lerned. If I try reel hard maybe Ill be a littel bit smarter then I was befor the operashun. I got my rabits foot and my luky penny and maybe they will help me.

If you ever reed this Miss Kinnian dont be sorry for me Im glad I got a second chanse to be smart becaus I lerned a lot of things that I never even new were in this world and Im grateful that I saw it all for a littel bit. I dont know why Im dumb agen or what I did wrong maybe its becaus I dint try hard enuff. But if I try and practis very hard maybel Ill get a littl smarter and know what all the words are. I remember a littel bit how nice I had a feeling with the blue book that has the torn cover when I red it. Thats why Im gonna keep trying to get smart so I can have that feeling agen. Its a good feeling to know things and be smart. I wish I had it rite now if I did I would sit down and reed all the time. Anyway I bet Im the first dumb person in the world who ever found out somthing importent for sience. I remember I did somthing but I dont remember what. So I gess its like I did it for all the dumb pepul like me.

Good-by Miss Kinnian and Dr Strauss and evreybody. And P.S. please tell Dr Nemur not to be such a grouch when pepul laff at him and he woud have more frends. Its easy to make frends if you let pepul laff at you. Im going to have lots of frends where I go.

P.P. S.   Please if you get a chanse put some flowrs on Algernons grave in the bak yard . . . .

QUESTIONS AND EXPLORATIONS

1 Keeping Track

Teaser

1 What does Charlie's opening speech suggest about his character?
2 Why do you think he speaks the way he does?
3 What is likely to happen next?

Scene 1

4 Do you detect any tension between the characters? If so, what do you think might be causing it?

Scene 2

5 'Maybe they won't use me'
   For what? (Look at Scene 1 again).
6 What further information about Charlie are we given?

Scene 3

7 What is Charlie's attitude to his own condition?
8 What will 'be temporary'? Why might this fact be important?

Scene 5

9 Why do you think Algernon wins the races in the maze?

Scene 6

10 'If the operation succeeds'
   What differences of attitude do you detect between Dr Nemur and Dr Strauss?

Scene 7

11 What is Charlie's motivation?

12 What have we learnt of Miss Kinnian's character so far?

Scene 8

13 'and be like other people'
An average IQ (intelligence quotient) is 100. Now look back at Scene 6. If the operation succeeds do you think Charlie will be like other people?

Scene 9

14 Do you notice anything different in the way that Charlie speaks now? Compare previous taped reports.

Scene 10

15 What attitudes does Charlie demonstrate here that have not been revealed before? Why do you think his attitude is changing?

Scene 11

16 Why, do you think, is the question 'Is Algernon going to stay smart permanent' *not* answered?

Scene 12

17 What are the attitudes of Charlie's workmates towards him? If his intelligence does improve, how are their attitudes likely to change?

Scene 13

18 Comment on the way that Dr Strauss treats Charlie.
19 'Your're getting smarter all the time. You just won't notice for a while'. What changes have *you* noticed?
20 What do you think the machine that Dr Strauss gives Charlie is?

Scene 14

21 What effect do you think Charlie's increasing intelligence is having on his happiness?

Scene 15

22 Although Charlie wins, he is upset for Algernon. What does this tell you about his character?

Scene 16

23 What is Miss Kinnian upset about?

Scene 18

24 What did Miss Kinnian say in Scene 16 that relates to the events in this scene? How do you feel towards Charlie's workmates here?

Scene 19

25 What evidence do you have about Charlie's growing independence of thought and behaviour?

Scene 21

26 'Joe and Frank are very uneasy with the new Charlie'. Why?

Scenes 22–23

27 What differences of opinion are evident between Dr Nemur and Dr Strauss?

Scene 24

28 What does Miss Kinnian explain to Charlie about his improving intelligence?
29 What are his feelings about what she says?
30 How have we been prepared for his announcement that he is in love with Miss Kinnian?

Scene 25

31 Why do you think the factory workers want Charlie to leave? Look at the end of Scene 20 for one suggestion.

Scene 26

32 What are Charlie's opinions about Dr Nemur and Dr Strauss?

33 What tone of voice does he use when speaking to them?

34 How do the two doctors respond to his accusations?

35 Could the 'strange look on Dr Strauss's face' mean something else?

36 Do you think Charlie's emotional development and social skills have kept pace with his intellectual development?

Scene 27

37 Look at the speech beginning 'Nemur seems to think that he hasn't so much helped me as created me'. Is Charlie right? Give evidence from what you have read so far.

Scene 28

38 'His smile freezes. He's very shaken'. Why?

Scene 29

39 Why has the meeting with the boy in the cafe been important to Charlie?

Scene 30

40 What reservations might Dr Nemur have other than the one Charlie picks up?

Scene 31

41 Why is the fact that Algernon bites Charlie important?

42 Why is he determined to go on with Dr Nemur's and Dr Strauss's research?

Scene 33

43 Charlie is very sure about his findings.
What are they?
44 What are his feelings about them?

Scene 35

45 Algernon is only a mouse.
Why does Charlie cry?

Scene 36

46 'I w-want you to l-leave me alone! G-go away!'
This is a turning point in the play.
Why is this moment so important?
47 Explain clearly what Charlie is saying in his final report
at the end of Scene 36.

Scenes 37 and 38

48 Explain as clearly as you can how Charlie feels about his
deterioration.
How have these changes been shown to us?

Scene 39

49 'I didn't want her to laugh at me like I remember her
doing before'.
Is he correct? Look back at Scene 28. Why *did* she laugh?
50 How does Mrs Flynn respond to him now?
51 How is further deterioration in Charlie shown in the
progress report?
52 Charlie says that the 'strange doctor' was making fun of
him. Do you think that he was? If not, how would you
explain his behaviour?

Scene 40

53 How do you explain Joe and Frank's attitude towards
Charlie now?

Why do they feel sorry for him?
54 'I'm going to have lots of frends where I go'. Why?
55 What are his intentions now? How does he feel about what happened to him?
56 How do *you* feel about Charlie now?
57 How do *you* feel about the whole experiment?

2 Explorations

A Characters

Charlie

1 Explain the changes that occur in Charlie from Scene 9 until the beginning of the regression in Scene 36.
2 'He said I had a good motor-vation'.
Using the whole play, show how Charlie's motivation is revealed to us and how it alters as the story unfolds.
3 What are Charlie's responses to, and understanding of, the following BEFORE the operation and AFTER the operation:
   a other people's treatment of and attitudes to him
   b his ability to perform various tasks
   c Miss Kinnian
   d Dr Strauss
   e Dr Nemur
   f Algernon
4 'I can't communicate with anyone very much now' (Scene 28)
Why does Charlie find it so difficult to communicate at the height of his intelligence?
5 Throughout the play, Charlie is lonely and isolated. Is this true? In what ways do the loneliness and the isolation alter?
6 Dr Strauss listens to all of Charlie's progress reports after he has gone away at the end of the play. From them, he compiles a magazine article about Charlie's

experiences to be published in a magazine for
psychologists.
Write the magazine article.

7 'I'll be able to read better and spell the words good and
know lots of things *and be like other people*'.
Charlie is never like other people. In what ways?

8 'I should tell more about what I feel and think'.
Charlie's intelligence was improved, but no-one really
understood his feelings and emotions. Do you agree?

9 'I think of my mother and father a lot these days'
Look at the last speech of Scene 38 and the entry for
July 7 in the original short story. What do you think
Charlie's childhood was like? How was he treated by his
parents?
What do you think happened to Charlie between the
time of his childhood and the age of 37 (the beginning
of the play)?

Miss Kinnian

1 Re-read Scene 16. Re-tell the scene from Miss
Kinnian's point of view, paying particular attention to
what she is thinking and feeling.

2 'I just hope I wasn't wrong, advising you to go into this
in the first place.' (Scene 24)
Miss Kinnian is beginning to have her doubts about
the wisdom of Charlie's going through with the
operation. What has caused her to have these doubts?

3 How is Miss Kinnian a constant support to Charlie
throughout the play? Find some of the things that she
says or does which are designed to help, support and
guide Charlie.

4 'Hello Miss Kinnian. Im redy for my lesin today only I
lost my book that we was using. She startid to cry and
run out of the room' (Scene 40).
Write Miss Kinnian's diary entry the next day. In it she
explains why she was so upset and looks back over what

happened to Charlie from the time just before the operation.

5   Is Miss Kinnian in any way responsible for what happened to Charlie?

Dr Nemur

1   'Nemur seems to think that he hasn't so much helped me as created me – to him I'm just a test result'. Examine this statement by going through the play and showing how Dr Nemur regards Charlie and the experiment as a whole.

2   Do you have any sympathy for Dr Nemur? Give evidence for your opinion.

3   Dr Nemur records his own progress report as the action of the play unfolds. Write some of the entries in which he explains what he thinks and feels about what is happening. Base your extracts on Scenes 6, 17, 22, 23, 26.

(You could re-read the original short story and use any further information about Dr Nemur to help you).

4   Write an additional scene to the play to be inserted after Scene 23. Imagine that word *has* got out about the experiment.

Dr Nemur is interviewed for a radio programme. Write the interview that he gives in which he explains, as confidently as he can, about the stages leading to Charlie's success.

(You could also include his private thoughts as a contrast to what he says to the interviewer. These would be spoken close to the microphone to convey the fact that he is thinking as opposed to speaking.)

Dr Strauss

1   Dr Strauss is a gifted surgeon but he has not thought through the possible consequences of his experimental

brain surgery. Do you agree?

2   Dr Strauss tries very hard to be supportive of and kind towards Charlie. Find all the evidence that demonstrates this.

3   Dr Strauss decides to believe Charlie's conclusion that the increasing of intelligence by artificial means has no practical application. He writes his final, formal report for the medical profession informing them of what he did and what he observed in Charlie.
Then he adds to his personal journal in which he says what he feels about the whole experience now that it is over.

4   Re-read Scene 6. From the conversation here it could be argued that Dr Strauss was at fault to insist on the operation going ahead and Dr Nemur was right to delay. Do you agree?

Frank and Joe

1   'He's got more guts than you'll ever have' (Joe – Scene 40). What has caused Frank and Joe to be so supportive of Charlie and to alter the ways that they treat him?

2   People like Frank, Joe and others at the factory need educating about mental handicap and the ways to respond to those who have problems like those of Charlie.
How *should* they have treated Charlie, and why?

3   'Before, when they laughed at me, they despised me for my ignorance; now, they hate me for my knowledge. What in God's name do they want of me?' (Scene 25) What *do* they want of him?

General

1   'No-one I've ever known is what he appears to be on the surface.'
Examine the characters of the play in the light of this statement.

2   Create and write a scene that shows Charlie trying to
    cope with life a few weeks after the end of the play.
3   Choose one of the following:
    Miss Kinnian; Mr Donnegan; Mrs Flynn; Bert;
    Professor Sherrinford.
    Write a monologue for your selected character set
    immediately after the end of the play which shows the
    character's attitudes and opinions about Charlie's case.
    Pay attention to characterisation, vocabulary and
    expression.
4   Create and write a scene set before the play begins. In
    this scene, Dr Nemur and Dr Strauss discuss their ideas
    in triple someone's intelligence through surgery. Try to
    include why they want to do this and what they think
    the long-term effects on an individual and the world in
    general will be. Remember to consult the character
    notes at the beginning of the play so that your
    characterisation is accurate.

B Themes

1   Supposing the operation had improved Charlie's
    intelligence enough to give him a 'normal' IQ, would
    your reactions to what Dr Nemur and Dr Strauss did
    to Charlie have been the same?
2   There is a great pressure on everyone to conform – to
    be like everyone else.
    In as much detail as you can, identify the different
    kinds of prejudice revealed in this play.
3   *Flowers for Algernon* reveals the need for tolerance and
    understanding in society. Which scenes highlight this
    need?
4   There will always be those who are superior and those
    who are inferior. What light does *Flowers for Algernon*
    cast on this statement?
5   What is the difference between intelligence and

wisdom? Examine the varying amounts of these qualities revealed by the major characters of the play.

6 What does this play have to say about love, friendship and loneliness?

Comparing the short story and the play

1 In the short story look carefully at Charlie's progress reports for March 5 and 6, April 13–18 and May 18. In the play look carefully at Scenes 1 and 2, 13–18 and 28. Analyse the different ways we are shown Charlie's improvement through his language. Comment on his spelling, punctuation, choice of words, sentence structure and any other features that you think are important.

2 What further information about Dr Nemur are we given in the short story? (Look, for example, at the entries made on April 27 and May 15). Does this information help you to understand his character and behaviour more than you are able to do through reading the play?

3 Look at the entry made on April 30 in the short story. Why didn't Fanny Girden sign the petition to fire Charlie?
Her comments are extremely profound and add something to the short story that the play lacks. Do you agree?

4 Bert Coules, who adapted this short story, writes:
' . . . you'll notice that I've changed the odd thing here and there.'
Re-read the short story and the play. List the details that have been changed or omitted altogether. Discuss why the changes or omissions have been made and whether you think they are effective.

GLOSSARY

Scene 1

IQ – intelligence quotient
the ratio, commonly expressed as a percentage, of a person's mental age to his actual age.

muscular co-ordination
the ability to move the body in general, and limbs in particular, in a balanced, harmonious way.

Scene 6

base intelligence
the recorded IQ of an individual.

Scene 7

psychologist
a person who studies the mind and behaviour and why people behave as they do.

Scene 14

subconscious
dimly conscious; away from the focus of attention.

unconscious
the deepest, inaccessible level of the mind.

Scene 15

ecstatic
an adjective describing the feeling of excessive joy, enthusiasm or exaltation.

sobers
becomes serious.

Scene 16

poring
gazing with close and steady attention.

afflicting
distressing.

Scene 19

tentatively
hesitantly, experimentally.

retarded
slow in development; having made less than normal progress in learning.

Scene 23

neurosurgery	operations on the nervous system commonly taking the form of a procedure carried out on the brain.

Scene 26

shackled	hampered, hindered.
analysis *psychoanalysis*	techniques used to explore a person's feelings, emotions and behaviour to discover their underlying cause.
inferiority complex	a state in which the individual feels personally inferior to another or others in general.
refute	to disprove.

Scene 30

designated	planned; assigned.

Scene 33

taken a liberty	presumed; given oneself the right to do something.
deteriorates	grows worse.
proportional	in direct relation to or ratio with.
inherent	existing in and inseparable from something else.
stability	state of being steady, balanced or fixed.
motor activity	movement of the body and limbs.
progressive amnesia	gradual inability to remember what has occurred.
syndromes	a characteristic pattern or group of symptoms.
irrefutable	cannot be disproved.
irrationality	that which is not reasonable, sane, intelligent.

Scene 38

'Uber psychische Ganzheit'	About psychological unity/wholeness .

FURTHER READING

Daniel Keyes *Flowers for Algernon* (the novel)
The novel is published in the UK by Heinemann
Educational in the New Windmill Series, Victor Gollancz
and Macmillan and in the USA by Boston Books Inc.

Aldous Huxley *Brave New World*
G R Kesteven *The Awakening Water*
George Orwell *1984*
Henry Sleasar (short story) *Examination Day*
John Wyndham *The Midwich Cuckoos*

Film
Charly (film of *Flowers for Algernon*)
Awakenings dir Penny Marshall
Enfant Sauvage dir Francois Truffaut
The Enigma of Kasper Hauser dir Werner Herzog

 **OTHER TITLES IN THIS SERIES**

Joyriders and Did You Hear The One about The Irishman? Age 14+

Christina Reid

'Mighty Belfast' is the setting for these two plays by Belfast-born playwright, Christina Reid. *Joyriders* is a hard-hitting play about four teenagers from the Divis flats in West Belfast, working on a youth scheme. Through jaunty, tense and often very funny dialogue the teenagers reveal their aspirations and dreams. In *Did You Hear the One About the Irishman?* Alison and Brian's families are linked by marriage but deeply divided by religion. Alison and Brian are warned that their relationship is dangerous but choose to ignore the threat to their lives . . .

This edition has notes and assignments to help in meeting the requirements of Key Stage 4.

ISBN: 435 23292 4

Confusions

Alan Ayckbourn

Confusions is a collection of five short interlinked but
self-contained plays with three to five male and female
characters in each. All deal with human loneliness and
hypocrisy in styles ranging from comic naturalism to
high farce.

The plays could be studied separately or together for
GCSE or A Level English Literature. This edition
provides notes, questions and assignments for both
levels.

ISBN: 0435 23300 9

A Taste of Honey

Age 14+

Shelagh Delaney

A new edition of this popular classic play about the complex, conflict ridden relationship between a teenage girl and her mother, and the fleeting moments of affection and escape she finds.

This edition provides notes and assignment suggestions for GCSE.

ISBN: 0435 23299 1

The Best Years Of Your Life & Lives Worth Living

Age 14+

Clive Jermain
Lawrence Evans
Jane Nash

Each of these plays offers frank, perceptive and sometimes humorous insights into the life of a disabled person.

In *The Best Years of Your Life* Robert has cancer of the spine. As a former star of the local football team he finds it difficult to meet his friends while sitting in a wheelchair. Throughout the play, Robert, his father and his brother, work out how to come to terms with his condition.

In *Lives Worth Living* Julie and her mentally-handicapped brother, Mark, are visiting the beach. during one short afternoon we see the whole range of joys and problems being with Mark involves. Through the livley, amusing dialogue between Julie and Mark we see the strong, mutual affection between them.

ISBN: 0435 23294 0

Solomon's Cat

Age 10+

David Holman

After Solomon frees a baby leopard from a trap on his way to school he knows he will do anything to protect the leopards from poachers. He is overjoyed when the ranger asks him to help look after the National Park. But protecting the leopards is no easy task. Many of the poachers are poor village farmers – the fathers of Solomon's friends – and the men who buy the skins are armed and dangerous. Solomon knows he is not just protecting the leopards but the whole future of wildlife in Tanzania and, against the odds, he takes incredible risks . . .

ISBN: 0435 23297 5